T0190534

JOSEPH FIELDING SMITH

Introductions to Mormon Thought

Edited by Matthew Bowman and Joseph M. Spencer
*For a list of books in the series, please see our website
at* www.press.uillinois.edu.

JOSEPH FIELDING SMITH

SMITH

A Mormon Theologian

MATTHEW BOWMAN

UNIVERSITY OF ILLINOIS PRESS
Urbana, Chicago, and Springfield

Library of Congress Cataloging-in-Publication Data
Names: Bowman, Matthew Burton, author.
Title: Joseph Fielding Smith : a Mormon theologian /
    Matthew Bowman.
Other titles: Introductions to Mormon thought.
Description: Urbana : University of Illinois Press,
    [2024] | Series: Introductions to Mormon thought
    | Includes bibliographical references and index.
Identifiers: LCCN 2023056327 (print) | LCCN
    2023056328 (ebook) | ISBN 9780252045950
    (cloth) | ISBN 9780252088056 (paperback) | ISBN
    9780252047138 (ebook)
Subjects: LCSH: Smith, Joseph Fielding, 1876–1972.
    | Church of Jesus Christ of Latter-day Saints—
    Presidents—Biography. | Theologians—United
    States—20th century—Biography. | Public
    historians—United States—20th century—
    Biography. | LCGFT: Biographies.
Classification: LCC BX8695.S64 B69 2024 (print) |
    LCC BX8695.S64 (ebook) | DDC 289.3092 [B]—
    dc23/eng/20240224
LC record available at https://lccn.loc.gov/2023056327
LC ebook record available at https://lccn.loc.gov/
    2023056328

Contents

Foreword to the Introductions to Mormon Thought Series

Our purpose in this series is to provide readers with accessible and short introductions to important figures in the intellectual life of the religious movement that traces its origins to the prophetic career of Joseph Smith Jr. With an eye to the many branches of that movement (rather than solely to its largest branch, the Church of Jesus Christ of Latter-day Saints), the series gathers studies of what scholars have long called *Mormon* thought. We define "thought" and "intellectual life," however, quite as broadly as we define "Mormonism." We understand these terms to be inclusive, not simply of formal theological or scholarly work, but also of artistic production, devotional writing, institutional influence, political activism, and other nonscholarly pursuits. In short, volumes in the series assess the contributions of men and women who have shaped how those called Mormons in various traditions think about what "Mormonism" is.

We hope that this series marks something of a coming of age of scholarship on this religious tradition. For many years, Mormon studies have focused primarily on historical questions largely of internal interest to the (specifically) Latter-day Saint community. Such historical work has furthermore mainly addressed the nineteenth century. Scholars have accordingly established the key sources for the study of Mormon history and culture, and they have established a broad consensus on many issues surrounding the origins and character of the religious movement. Recent work, however, has pushed academics into the work of comparison, asking larger questions in two key ways. First, recent scholars have approached these topics from a greater variety of disciplines. There has emerged in Mormon studies, in other words, increasing visibility for the disciplines of philosophy, sociology, literary criticism, and media studies, among others. Second, scholars working this field have also begun to consider new topics of study—in particular gender and sexuality, the status of international Mormonism, and the experience of minority groups within the tradition. We believe the field has thus reached the point where the sort of syntheses these books offer is both possible and needed.

While key contributions to the series so far have examined—and many key contributions still to come will yet examine—historical figures at some distance from the institutional center of the Latter-day Saint faith, Matthew Bowman's study trains its focus on a company man: Joseph Fielding Smith. The grandnephew of Mormonism's founder, an apostle and then a president of the Church of Jesus Christ of Latter-day Saints, the official historian of the Church for decades, and a toweringly influential author, Fielding Smith represents the very mainstream of mid-twentieth-century Mormonism. Precisely for that reason, however, representatives of the field of Mormon studies, which today rests on intellectual foundations that were laid when Smith's institutional and intellectual influence was at its peak, have more often than not reacted to rather than reflected on the man. Bowman's investigation of Fielding Smith's intellectual background, careful examination of his style of thought, and exploration of his place in the flow of American religious history broadly—all this encapsulates what it means to reassess the current shape of Mormon intellectual culture, and especially of its relationship to the larger context in which it is situated. Embracing the vital task of reexamining the center of the tradition, alongside other volumes that work to expand the margins of the tradition, Bowman's study is an especially welcome contribution to *Introductions to Mormon Thought*.

Matthew Bowman
Joseph M. Spencer

Acknowledgments

I owe thanks to the Special Collections staff at the Marriott Library at the University of Utah and the Lee Library at Brigham Young University, particularly Cindy Brightenburg. Thanks also to Ben Whisenant and Jen Barkdull at the LDS Church History Library and Archives.

This project began as an idle chat with Joe Spencer at SLAB Pizza in Provo, Utah; I'm delighted how far it's come, and appreciative of Joe's thoughtfulness, insights, and labor.

Thanks to my family as well. This one's for Bean.

JOSEPH FIELDING SMITH

CHAPTER ONE

An Intellectual Life

One of the earliest, and worst, memories of Joseph Fielding Smith's life was the terrible Christmas of 1884. He was eight years old. On December 18, 1884, six days before Christmas Eve, young Fielding Smith sat in the parlor of his family's rambling home three blocks west of Temple Square in Salt Lake City with his many brothers and sisters, his mother, and his four "aunties"—his father's plural wives.

His father, Joseph F. Smith, then a counselor in the First Presidency of the Church of Jesus Christ of Latter-day Saints, gave each person in the room a farewell blessing, one by one. He and Fielding Smith's mother Julina were fleeing Salt Lake City for Hawai'i. There his father would preside over the Church in the Pacific islands, and both he and Julina would be safe from the federal marshals who were descending on the Utah Territory hunting for polygamists. They were gone for years. It was not until 1890, when the Church formally renounced plural marriage and 1894, when President Grover Cleveland finally pardoned its practitioners, that Joseph Fielding Smith could feel his family was safe, and his father permanently settled home again.

As it was, for the rest of his life he remembered well his anger at those who persecuted his church and drove his parents away. He insisted, always, on dichotomies. "We lived a very peaceful and happy family life except when we became troubled and I became frightened by deputy marshals," he remembered later.[1] He also recalled vividly the raids. On February 7, 1885, young Joseph Fielding Smith was home when four federal marshals knocked on the door, forced their way into the house, and separated one of the aunties and five children for interrogation. For years, the boy was

2

terrified that the marshals would return. "Well and long will they be remembered by those children who were home and forced to listen to the abuse and the threats," he wrote bitterly fifty years later.[2]

Joseph Fielding Smith (whom I will refer to as "Fielding Smith" to distinguish him from his father and great-uncle, Joseph Smith, the founder of the church that dominated all their lives) was born on July 19, 1876, and would live until 1972, dying at the age of ninety-five. He served as an apostle of his church, one of its fifteen highest leaders, for a full sixty years, Church historian and recorder for forty-nine, and president for two. During those decades, he defended the Church and changed it in the defending. His primary mode of defense was writing. He produced more than two dozen books and many, many articles over his long life. For nearly two decades, he maintained in the Church's primary magazine a column called "Your Question," in which he took religious inquiries from lay members of the Church and answered hundreds.

His son-in-law, Bruce R. McConkie, once speculated that "no man in this dispensation has traveled more miles, attended more meetings, preached more sermons, performed more ordinances, or written more voluminously."[3] It is quite possible, given the rapid growth of the Church in Fielding Smith's lifetime and his nearly seven decades of writing, preaching, and traveling, that McConkie was correct.

Because he was so prolific and so long-lived and so widely read and influential, Joseph Fielding Smith was without question the most important Latter-day Saint theologian of the twentieth century. And the content and the style of his theology—defensive, insistent on certainty, particularity, and exclusivity—was that of the boy whose parents were ripped from him in the 1880s.

This is not to say that Fielding Smith's theology could be reduced simply to a reaction to traumatic experience. But certainly his perception of the world around him was framed in part by what that experience represented. His service as a missionary in the British Isles from 1899 to 1901, for instance, was a bitter experience that confirmed for him that the world was a hostile place. His letters and diaries report a mission made up of combative encounters, little sympathy from the British, and no converts. He arrived in Nottingham, England, on June 4, 1899, at the age of twenty-two. According to his journal, no one was there to meet him at the train station. So he gathered his baggage himself and found his way to the mission headquarters. The place was closed, locked, and empty. Young Fielding Smith parked his luggage in the doorway and began wandering back and forth on the street, wondering where his fellow church members were. "I traveled alone, in a strange land, and among a strange people, where I would have little or no sympathy if I were known," he wrote in his journal. And indeed, once passersby were able to identify him as a member of the Church by virtue of his lingering at the mission home, he began to suffer teasing from a group of boys in the street, who sang a snippet of a taunting song.[4]

It got no better. As a missionary, he repeatedly suffered dismissal, argument, and rejection. Later in life, he told a grandson that he was once threatened with a knife.[5] By the time he had been in England several months, he had become convinced that, as he wrote in his journal, "The best blood of Israel has long since been gathered out of this land."[6] At the six-month mark, he assured his sister Rachel, twelve years younger than himself, that "You would not like to live here, I know." He expressed wistfulness about the absence of the mountains that towered over Salt Lake City, asked plaintively about the rest of their siblings, and added that British children did not seem so happy to him as did the boys and girls of his own family. "Their Papas and Mommas do not love them so much as our Papa and Momma loves us," he wrote.[7]

Certainly, Fielding Smith's experience on his mission only reinforced his perception of the world as essentially unfriendly. But Fielding Smith's thought was deeply marked by other factors as well.

Family

One such factor was his own identity as a Smith, a member of the founding family of his faith. The persecution of his family made him all the more compelled to manifest loyalty to their legacy, or at least what he perceived that legacy to be. Perhaps in response to the raids, Fielding Smith began to lionize his male ancestors as beacons of hope in a depraved world. His biography of his father makes clear what a hero Fielding Smith understood the man to be—a vision perhaps intensified because of the man's so-frequent absence. Though he returned to Utah when Fielding Smith was a teenager, Joseph F. became president of the Church in 1901, and again his duties pulled him from his family. "During those years when a boy needs the counsel of his father the most, I had no father," Fielding Smith wrote.[8]

And yet, the boy loved his father desperately. In a biography of his father he produced twenty years after the man's death, Fielding Smith wrote, "The wicked and the depraved have ridiculed and maligned him; but the true condition of his family life and wonderful love for his family is beyond their comprehension." He linked that love to loyalty to the Church. He remembered his father saying that "I would rather take one of my children to the grave than I would see him turn away from this Gospel."[9]

It was not only his immediate family that had such a hold on him. Upon Fielding Smith's return from his mission in England, his father secured for him a position in the Church Historian's Office. Almost immediately, he began work researching the Smith family. In July 1902, he traveled to Massachusetts to research the ancestry of his great-uncle Joseph Smith Jr., founding prophet of the Church. The trip produced his first publication, a small study of Joseph Smith's grandfather Asahel Smith.[10] It also seems to have set the stage for the rest of his life. His church, which taught that the living could perform saving ordinances like baptism by proxy for their dead, set great stock on interest in the history of one's family.

In 1906, Fielding Smith became an assistant church historian and returned to Boston to follow up on his earlier research. He wrote to his father how impressed he was with the genealogical societies he encountered. He marveled that "Everywhere societies have been built up in New England and great sums endowed for Genealogical purposes." It shamed him, in fact. He worried that Church members had "failed to donate anything for the salvation of the dead even of their own line."[11] In 1908, he became director and librarian of the Genealogical Society of Utah, a new Church-affiliated organization formed to aid in family history work. While polygamy had bonded the Saints together horizontally to others, genealogy and work for the dead began to create a church that extended vertically through time. Fielding Smith was committed to the work, so much so that he often funded the society from his own pocket. In 1921, he was named the Church historian, and in 1934 president of the Genealogical Society.[12]

His grandfather, Joseph F.'s father, was Hyrum Smith, brother of Church founder Joseph Smith. Both were killed by a mob in 1844, a story young Joseph Fielding Smith heard throughout his life, alongside the stories of his grandmother's flight to the Salt Lake Valley with her children, which followed the murders. He wrote once to a friend that "one thing that has impelled me onward is that I am justly proud of my ancestry." He reminisced about his grandfather Hyrum Smith, "a martyr because he held jointly with his younger brother the keys of this dispensation. How can I betray him?" He described his own father's life "of hardship and deprivation until middle life and in later years was abused by his enemies as few men have been abused, because he loved the truth. How can I fail him?"[13] When he was grown, he kept in his study a rocking chair that had belonged to Hyrum Smith.[14]

Fielding Smith received two patriarchal blessings, special blessings given to members of the Church for counsel and guidance by men who were, in Fielding Smith's day, directly descended from the family of Joseph Smith himself. Fielding Smith heard in his blessings confirmation of the significant role he had inherited from his family. The first, given when he was nineteen by his uncle John Smith, promised him he would be "a mighty man in Israel" and enjoined him to "reflect often on the past, present and future." His later blessing, received when he was nearly forty, was more specific. Given by his cousin Joseph D. Smith, it instructed Fielding Smith that the "evidence you have gathered will stand as a wall of defense against those who are seeking and will seek to destroy the evidence of the divinity of the mission of the prophet Joseph."[15] His lineage meant to him a responsibility, sometimes burdensome.

The devotion he bore for his ancestors and the pain it caused him was reflected in his own family life. He was married and widowed three times. He married his first wife, Louisa (Louie) Shurtliff, when he was twenty-two, only a few months before he was sent on his mission. The daughter of a friend of his father, she lived with the Smith family while she attended the University of Utah and insisted on graduating before she would marry him. She died in March 1908, only three months before her thirty-second birthday, of complications with her third pregnancy. Fielding Smith was left a thirty-one-year-old single father of two daughters. He moved back into his father's house, and his mother Julina and his aunties helped care for his children. He wrote later that his father-in-law, his mother, and his father urged him to remarry quickly.[16]

He began to court Ethel Reynolds and six months later married her, a nineteen-year-old clerk in the Church Historian's Office. After their marriage, he wrote to her, "How thankful I am that you were sent to me in the hour of trial and my need. . . . I do feel a little tender just now."[17] They had nine children together over the next twenty years, and in 1924 he built his increasingly large family a new home on Douglas Street in Salt Lake City, in a leafy neighborhood on the eastern foothills of the Salt Lake Valley a few miles south of Church headquarters at Temple Square. His children remembered him as an active parent, always the first out of bed to start the furnace in the morning. He would write early in the mornings while the house was warming up and late at night after his family retired to bed, in order to spend as much time with them as possible. He insisted on music lessons for the family and enjoyed playing sports with his children. (When some sons served in the army during World War II, Fielding Smith sent them regular letters describing University of Utah football games.) According to one daughter, he never resorted to physical punishment. He always kissed each child on the cheek upon greetings and departure, a practice that became embarrassing to them as they grew up.[18]

In the 1930s, Ethel began to deteriorate mentally and then physically. One of her sons wrote that she suffered "a terrible illness which she could not understand. At times she was plunged into the depths of depression and at other times her mind raced beyond control." She became unable to cope with the various demands made on her time and was released from her administrative positions in the Church. Meanwhile, Fielding Smith's responsibilities in the Church were increasing, and he left her more and more to administer the Church across the United States and the world. Ethel was less and less able to accompany him. In his journal for August 26, 1937, he wrote that he rushed home from his office "to the bedside of my wife who was suddenly stricken. . . . [S]he has been ailing for many months, and in spite of all aid passed away at 3:15 today. A better woman could not be found." She had suffered a cerebral hemorrhage. She was forty-seven years old; they had been married for twenty-eight years.[19]

Ethel, when she sensed that her condition was worsening, had requested that Jessie Evans, a popular soloist who sang with the Mormon Tabernacle Choir, perform at her funeral, which she did. Afterward, Fielding Smith wrote to thank her, and correspondence evolved between the two. In December 1937, Fielding Smith proposed and she accepted. They married the next year, and though Fielding Smith outlived her too, their marriage was his longest. Jessie died in August 1971, after nearly thirty-three years of marriage and only a year before Fielding Smith himself. She had borne no children, but her stepchildren called her Aunt Jessie, just as Fielding Smith had called his father's other wives.

The nickname soon spread among Church members, and as her husband rose in prominence so did Jessie Evans Smith. The stories that circulated about her sly wittiness made her and her husband's personalities legendary. In these stories, she would gesture to her neckline and tell reporters that she was wearing her "Bible dress—low and behold." Or she would interrupt a long and stern sermon by her husband on the Second Coming of Jesus, saying loudly from her seat "Joseph, just tell them when He's coming!" Her ebullience and sense of humor threw a contrast onto his dour public image; she was capable of drawing him out and giving him room to express his own wry sense of humor. She claimed to have made him practice the piano so they could sing together and was willing to tease him in public.[20]

Soon after their marriage, Fielding Smith's son Lewis was killed while serving in the army during World War II. His father was in agony. He sent multiple letters to his other serving son, Douglas, worried because he was receiving letters from Douglas that seemed to indicate the boy had not heard the news. "We are greatly troubled because you have not had our word concerning Lewis," he wrote, castigating the unreliable military mail. It took three letters before he received confirmation that Douglas knew about his brother's death. In Fielding Smith's first letter to Douglas on his brother's death, he compared the fallen Lewis to his grandfather, Hyrum Smith, also slain, and quoted Joseph Smith: "O how many are the sorrows we have shared together, and again we find ourselves shackled with the unrelenting land of oppression." He mourned that the war was the "product of iniquity of every kind, but ultimately celebrated that "Lewis was faithful to every trust. He did not betray his faith, he was true to every obligation." It was, as always, his confidence in the faith of his family that comforted him in his sufferings.[21]

Joseph Fielding Smith's family was both painfully distant and unbearably close his entire life.

The Intellectuals

As Joseph Fielding Smith rose through the ranks of the Church's leadership, a disjuncture became increasingly apparent.

Aside from his sojourn in England, Fielding Smith lived his entire life in Salt Lake City, Utah. He completed his formal education while a teenager with two years at the Latter-day Saint College, which provided the basics of a high school education—mathematics, spelling, grammar, history, and so on. This was more education than Hyrum or Joseph Smith had accomplished, and he believed it entirely sufficient. Describing his career to his son, he wrote, "I did not require a technical education for it."[22] When he took the job as official assistant historian of the Church, he had no formal qualifications and relied entirely on his tenacious, rigorous mind and unflagging capacity for work. He did much to professionalize the Church's archives, taking seriously his responsibility to educate himself about cataloguing and processing and archival techniques through his life.[23] And yet, when he began publishing in the first decade of the twentieth century the world was rapidly changing.

Those Church leaders often spoken of as Fielding Smith's intellectual peers, those who published at similar rates as he did and sometimes engaged in dispute and discussion with him, increasingly were the products of a modern educational world. The apostles John Widtsoe and James Talmage, for instance, both worked for decades with Fielding Smith and each produced works of theology as influential in their time as anything Fielding Smith wrote. Both men had been educated in universities outside Utah, both held PhDs in the sciences, and both read widely in the religious and philosophical literature of the time. Though some Latter-day Saint thinkers who engaged with Fielding Smith were no more formally educated than he was, like his colleague in the Genealogical Society, Susa Young Gates, or the Seventy B. H. Roberts—who emerged as Fielding Smith's most tenacious intellectual rival—they were deeply engaged with the intellectual conversations of the early-twentieth-century United States. Both traveled widely, read deeply, and, like Widtsoe and Talmage, sought to explain their faith in the fashionable intellectual language of their times.

The changes in the intellectual climate of the time accompanied broader transformations in American culture. In the late nineteenth century, American universities were self-consciously abandoning their older affiliation with (most frequently) Protestant denominations and pursuing a new way of thinking about and organizing knowledge—the ideal of professionalized academics. In this, American universities were imitating trends emerging from Germany, where universities had begun to grant the first doctoral degrees in the West and had begun to organize knowledge into disciplines like history, classics, literature, and science. As these processes developed, the idea of "expertise" began to take root in the United States. To study history, one must master the language and processes of the historian; to understand science, one required training, and so on. For some, such approaches to knowledge seemed to challenge older authorities—particularly religious leadership.[24]

Part of the work of figures like Talmage and Widtsoe, then, was to find ways to reconcile the changes with religious faith. They often did so by attempting to claim that these new disciplines of knowledge were always already part of religious belief—that there need be no conflict. And for some Latter-day Saints, their work was successful.[25]

Joseph Fielding Smith was an outlier to these trends, and he resented them. Rather than seeking alliances between older and newer forms of knowledge, he perceived the process as subverting and destroying the traditional forms of authority he had long prized—in particular, the lay authority of Church leaders such as his own family. The trends were part of a broader process of professionalization in many arenas in American life, but for Fielding Smith the changes felt quite personal. Much of his pastoral career became a matter of fighting a rearguard action, attempting to preserve what he believed to be the traditional beliefs of his faith. He identified "genuine" religion with that which he understood his father and grandfather to have taught; he perceived the work of Talmage, Widtsoe, and Roberts to be contaminated by outside ideas, and thus not pure. His relative physical isolation in Utah was matched by a conscious provincialism that he perceived as an act of boundary maintenance.

The embrace of professionalization and expertise in early-twentieth-century America is one useful way to conceive of what it meant then to be "modern." That is a term that means one thing to literary critics, another to cultural historians, another to sociologists. Scholars of US history like James Kloppenberg and Jackson Lears, influenced by theorists like Max Weber, describe modernity as the shape of a society confidently remaking itself after the Civil War. Modernity was not a neutral or impersonal process; rather, it reflected the values and interests of a new elite: academics, industrialists, journalists, writers, politicians. Modernity is the organization and regulation of society for the interests of efficiency and productivity invested with morality. And, of course, moderns celebrated all these things as advancement: the march of civilization, the triumph of progress.[26]

Antimodernists took on a variety of forms—but all were skeptical of conventional narratives of progress, civilization, and efficiency. The deeply gloomy historian Henry Adams, grandson and great-grandson of presidents, saw only rapaciousness in industrial America and mourned the reduction of its politicians from the stately and patrician figures of his own ancestry to figures like Ulysses Grant, to Adams an entirely mechanical thinker, a military tactician overwhelmed by the industrial forces at work in modern America. The social activist Vida Scudder found inspiration in the mystical world of medieval Catholicism, whose ordered and metaphysical society felt alive in a way the increasingly regulated and individualist world of industrial America did not.

Of course, among the best-known antimodernists are Protestant fundamentalists. The original inventors of the term *fundamentalist* were Baptists, who used it to describe adherence to a fundamental set of doctrines. More useful than a theological definition might be the *Fundamentalisms Project* of scholars Martin Marty and R. Scott Appleby, which interprets fundamentalism as a particularly modern religious response to modernity. That is, fundamentalism does not simply hold to traditional orthodoxies. Rather, it is a variety of antimodernism, particularly modern itself in its concerns and in the structure of its response. Like Adams, fundamentalists were pessimists about the moral state of an industrial society and, like Scudder, were believers in religious communities as a viable alternative to capitalist individualism.

Joseph Fielding Smith was a Mormon antimodernist. His fondness for the intellectual tropes of Protestant fundamentalism—like his young earth creationism, for instance—should be understood as derivative of a broader suspicion of modernity as he understood it: a professionalized world that seemed to leave behind the religious community his family had founded.

Career

In 1905, Fielding Smith's father asked him to write an essay taking on Richard Evans, a leader of the Reorganized Church of Jesus Christ of Latter Day Saints, who had published an interview in the *Toronto Star* besmirching, as the Smiths believed, the reputation of the LDS Church. The Reorganized Church had coalesced around the leadership of Joseph Smith's children a decade and a half after the prophet's murder, and after Brigham Young had led the bulk of Smith's followers to Salt Lake City. Reorganized leadership had always rejected distinctive LDS practices like polygamy and proxy

sacramental work for the dead and, in that way, sought to position themselves as a more respectable version of Mormonism. Thus, in a way, Evans
was a stand-in for a broader challenge. In 1905, the US Senate's deliberations
about whether to seat the LDS apostle Reed Smoot, whom Utah had elected
to serve in the federal body, were national news. Fielding Smith's father had
been forced to testify before the Senate, and both senators and the media
seemed skeptical of the Church. Fielding Smith ended up publishing two
booklets drawn from his exchanges with Evans, and his father placed him
on a special committee charged with "defense of the church." His spirited
defense of his faith raised his stature such that his father saw fit to make
Fielding Smith an apostle in 1910, an ecclesiastical position he balanced
with his positions in the Church Historian's Office.[27]

Fielding Smith's path seemed set. He spent his career as an apostle serving as the Church's leading official intellectual. On the one hand, he served
in a number of administrative positions governing the Church's intellectual
life. He was a longtime member of the General Church Board of Education
and chairman of the executive committee of the Brigham Young University Board of Trustees from 1939 until he became president of the Church
in 1970, a position that made him especially concerned for the Church's
educational efforts. In 1944, he became chairman of the Church's publications committee, reading all materials the Church proposed to use in its
educational programs and auxiliaries for doctrinal adequacy. He served in a
number of other capacities as well—as a member of the Melchizedek Priesthood committee, which oversaw the general administration of the Church,
in various leadership capacities in the Church's missionary program, and
for four years, from 1945 to 1949, as president of the Salt Lake Temple.
At the outbreak of World War II, he was posted in Europe to direct the
evacuation of missionaries from the continent. But it was those first roles,
in education and publication, which allowed him to enunciate and enforce
what he believed to be genuine LDS theology, in which he flourished.[28]

And, of course, he wrote. Many of the projects he took on were conscious
attempts to formulate a standard orthodoxy for the Church, a mandate he
believed his father had given him and one to which he believed himself, as
a Smith, particularly well suited. In 1920, he approached David O. McKay,
an apostle senior to him, by letter. Fielding Smith said that a number of
his friends had approached him suggesting that he was just the person to
write a short history of the Church. Just as significant as the suggestions

was the fact that Fielding Smith was worried that James E. Talmage would want the job. So Fielding Smith asked McKay to advocate for him before the Church president and, two years later, he published *Essentials in Church History*.[29] He followed that volume with others, the one as ambitious and comprehensive as the other. *The Way to Perfection* and *The Progress of Man* were both presented as exhaustive treatments of the story of humanity; the latter was quite explicitly a history from Adam and Eve to the present day and the former an explication of the story of human salvation. Intending both books to be manuals for the work of the Genealogical Society, Fielding Smith observed that the latter was intended to be "authoritative."[30]

In the years immediately after World War II, Fielding Smith was pursuing the same ends in the realm of theology. His most famous book, 1954's *Man: His Origin and Destiny*, was intended as a comprehensive rebuttal of the theory of organic evolution and of higher criticism of scripture. For more than twenty years, Fielding Smith had been periodically publishing answers to religious questions he received in the mail in the official newspaper, the *Church News*. In 1953, the editors of the *Improvement Era*, the largest and most widely read of the Church's periodicals, prevailed on Fielding Smith to turn the practice into a regular column. In the same decade, his son, Joseph Fielding Smith Jr., began to compile and issue more volumes of Fielding Smith's theological writings and, in 1957, the junior Smith began to issue volumes in a series called *Answers to Gospel Questions*.[31]

This impulse toward consolidation and systematization was characteristic of modernity. The late nineteenth and early twentieth century in the United States is sometimes called the Progressive Era, and it was a time of professionalization. In that era, drawing on the formalization of the US academy, professionals of all sorts began standardizing policies, procedures, and knowledge. It was the time in which states began requiring licensure for lawyers; the time in which medical schools began institutionalizing the profession; the time in which government agencies started regulating the US economy. Just so, Fielding Smith's father and other LDS writers like Talmage and Widtsoe had made their own attempts at collating and standardizing Church doctrine after the abandonment of polygamy.[32]

Protestant fundamentalists' attraction to the notion of systematized, standardized doctrine marks the way their antimodernism was particularly modern.[33] Certainly, Joseph Fielding Smith drew on the same impulses. One of Fielding Smith's best-known books, *Signs of the Times*, incorporated fundamentalist ideas about the end times.³⁴ Similarly, in the early 1930s, he and B. H. Roberts engaged in a protracted debate over the age of the earth and tangentially the theory of evolution. Roberts had submitted a work for approval and publication that accepted the possibility of life and death before the fall of Adam and Eve, and Fielding Smith roused himself, objecting in his role as member of the publications committee to presenting such ideas under Church auspices. Fielding Smith protested Roberts's work before the Quorum of the Twelve and the First Presidency of the Church and managed to prevent its publication. These actions, as much as Smith's written theological work, illustrated his concern for developing and preserving orthodoxy among Latter-day Saints. For Joseph Fielding Smith, being genuinely religious required one to believe in precise doctrine, and much of his work was designed to promote that idea.

As he said in one form or another frequently, "If I am wrong, then the revelations are wrong—I have not placed private interpretation upon them—but the same interpretation that the leading elders of the Church have placed upon them, including the prophet Joseph Smith."³⁵ For Fielding Smith, that "same interpretation" mandated an earth only a few thousand years old, no death on the earth before the fall of a real Adam and Eve, a global flood, and various other theological ideas gaining steam among conservative, or fundamentalist, Christians in the early-twentieth-century United States. But though Fielding Smith sympathized with many such ideas, he remained a virulent opponent of Protestant ideas about salvation and a staunch advocate for the exceptional nature of his church throughout his life. While fundamentalism blurred the lines between Protestant churches in early-twentieth-century America, for Fielding Smith doctrinal rigor also meant LDS exclusivity.

In particular, Fielding Smith sought to promote his ideas within the Church Education System. He had served as acting president of the Quorum of the Twelve Apostles under the presidency of George Albert Smith, from 1945 to 1951, and, as the longest-serving apostle, took the job in full when David O. McKay became Church president in 1951. The position invested him with more administrative power than he had held before. He was a strong advocate for developing a larger, stronger infrastructure of education within the Church, and, in his role as chairman of the executive committee of the Brigham Young University (BYU) Board of Trustees, he worked closely with the ambitious Ernest Wilkinson, who served as president of that university from 1951 to 1970. Both Wilkinson and Fielding Smith wanted to transform BYU into a large research university. They grew its student body and physical plant to that end. Wilkinson also shared Fielding Smith's allegiance not only to conservative theology, but to the need for orthodoxy. In the 1950s and 1960s, Wilkinson, allied with other Church leaders like Harold B. Lee, a young apostle and acolyte of Fielding Smith, and J. Reuben Clark, a member of the First Presidency who shared Fielding Smith's conservative tendencies (but bristled at the apostle's desire to make himself the arbiter of doctrine), began to centralize and transform Church education, forming in 1970 a consolidated "Church Education System." They targeted instructors they believed unorthodox, tightened the curriculum, and transformed the processes of hiring to favor teachers who shared their own ideas about orthodoxy. By the 1950s, they ended the so-called "Chicago experiment" in which Church teachers would receive graduate training in religion at the University of Chicago. Instead, hiring began to favor teachers trained only in Church schools.[36]

Fielding Smith himself had awkward confrontations with some such instructors. His interactions with educators with professional training in philosophy or religion like Heber Snell (whose book Fielding Smith judged unorthodox and banned from Church schools), Sterling McMurrin (who had left the Church's employ by the time he crossed Fielding Smith's path, but who represented much of what Fielding Smith feared), Lowell Bennion (who confronted Fielding Smith over issues of race and creationism) and others illustrated his willingness to both create and enforce doctrinal boundaries.

In 1965, David O. McKay, president of the Church, took the unusual step of expanding the First Presidency of the Church. Normally consisting of the president and two counselors, McKay added between 1965 and 1968 three more men, including Joseph Fielding Smith. The position did not add a great deal of responsibilities to Fielding Smith's shoulders. He continued serving as Church historian and continued the extensive travels to visit and oversee the arms of the Church around the world that had begun when he became President of the Quorum of the Twelve. But he began to join the regular meetings of the Church's highest leadership. That, along with the duties he took up as president of the Twelve, began to immerse him in the administrative work thar prepared him to take up the presidency in his own right.[37]

By the time he became president of the Church upon McKay's death in January 1970, Fielding Smith was ninety-three and, quite understandably, somewhat past his prime. He continued publishing—two volumes of sermons—but his intellectual legacy was already secured. By that point, many younger leaders of the Church, including the influential apostles Mark E. Petersen and Harold B. Lee, Fielding Smith's son-in-law Bruce McConkie, a rising member of the Seventy, the third rank of Church leadership, and a large number of BYU faculty considered Fielding Smith a mentor and the model of appropriate Latter-day Saint theology. The *Improvement Era*, the Church's leading magazine, claimed upon his ascension to the presidency that "No one has the detailed understanding of the law and doctrines underlying the government of the Church, together with such an extensive experience with its jurisprudence and organization, whether in its national or international setting, as has President Smith."[38]

His service as president lasted two and a half years, until his own death July 2, 1972, two weeks before his ninety-sixth birthday. Though he took up the mantle as president of the Church only a few days after McKay's death on January 18, 1970, he was sustained by the Church assembled in a General Conference on April 4, 1970—sixty years almost to the day since he had been sustained as an apostle on April 7, 1910. Notably, he returned the First Presidency to its most common configuration of a president and two counselors, removing the extra counselors McKay had called. He also elevated his own protégé Harold B. Lee to the First Presidency as his first counselor. Lee had not served McKay in that capacity, but he had a number of things to recommend him in Fielding Smith's eyes. The two were ideologically sympathetic. Lee was widely respected as a vigorous and talented administrator and was the next in line for the presidency of the Church. He was also twenty-three years younger than Fielding Smith.

Much of Fielding Smith's tenure as president was taken up less with the theological and intellectual work that had consumed so much of his apostolic career and more with the administrative demands of a growing, and increasingly internationalizing church. Lee had spent the previous decade mounting a movement that has come to be called the "correlation" of the Church—a large-scale reorganization and consolidation of administrative authority. Fielding Smith, whose world view and comprehension of what the Church of Jesus Christ of Latter-day Saints should be was so deeply marked by personal and familial bonds, was presiding over its bureaucratization and routinization.[39]

But Fielding Smith embraced the process. His travels had convinced him of the need for a more robust international organization. In August 1971, he traveled to Great Britain and spoke at the first "area conference" of the Church. These were smaller international gatherings that he had decided were needed to establish local organizations more firmly. "It is a matter of great satisfaction to me and my Brethren that the Church has now grown to the point that it seems wise and necessary to hold general conferences in various nations," he said.[40] During his presidency, the *Improvement Era* and the host of other Church magazines were consolidated into three general-purpose magazines intended for adults, young adults, and children, respectively. A large new Church office building was completed in Temple Square to house thousands of workers in the Church's new bureaucracy. And that bureaucracy was reorganized. The sort of work that Fielding Smith had done in running the Historian's Office for decades would no longer fall on apostles. Instead, the load of regular administration of various Church departments was given to a newly hired class of department managers and directors, reserving to apostles the task of supervision and pastoral work. The Historian's Office became the Church Historical Department; a public communications office was established; and a new internal communications department would now supervise Church publications and curriculum.

During all this reorganization, Fielding Smith suffered the last tragedies of his life. His wife Jessie, only sixty-nine years old, died after a short illness on August 3, 1971. Since she was so much younger than Fielding Smith himself, her passing was a terrible surprise, and it marked the beginning of his own physical decline. After Jessie's death, he moved in with his daughter Amelia and son-in-law Bruce R. McConkie. That autumn, he suffered pains and shortness of breath that incapacitated him for a week and, in December, he fell and broke a shoulder, some ribs, and a hip. The following July 2, he died quietly while resting in his favorite chair in his daughter's living room soon after the family had a light dinner.

Joseph Fielding Smith was the rare president of the Church of Jesus Christ of Latter-day Saints, one whose primary influence on the Church had little to do with his presidency. Had he never served in that office, his writings would have been equally influential. His works were widely read before he took that office and stayed so afterward. Many of his books—particularly

Essentials in Church History and *Man: His Origin and Destiny*—remained cited and used in official Church curricula for years after his death. In 1984, for instance, Ezra Taft Benson, who, in a matter of months, would become president of the Church, declared it "apparent to all who have the Spirit of God in them that Joseph Fielding Smith's writings will stand the test of time."[41]

Fielding Smith was a prime mover in the Church's drift toward theological conservatism in the late twentieth century; he moved from the fringes of the Church's intellectual life in his early years to its center by his death. But he was not simply an importer of conservative Protestant fundamentalist ideas—creationism, biblical inerrancy, and dispensationalism—into Mormonism. Rather, though he undoubtedly drew on fundamentalist writers, he read them through the lens of his fierce loyalty to the identity and theology he grew up with, and he reinterpreted fundamentalist theology in ways that made it distinctively his own.

CHAPTER TWO

Texts

One of the lengthiest of Joseph Fielding Smith's diary entries during his mission to the British Isles describes a confrontation that seems to be the high point of that otherwise dreary two-year affair. It was a debate with his landlord, and it was about the Bible. The landlord, a Mr. Blood, seemed to be trying to smooth over the differences between his young lodger's church and Blood's own. "We should not believe differently from anyone else in our foundation," the man said, arguing that all Christian churches rested on the same confidence in Jesus Christ, "although we might in church government."[1]

But to this, Joseph Fielding took exception. Soon, the two were tangled in a dispute that took two tracks. On the one hand, the apparently excitable Mr. Blood's "eyes bulged out" when Joseph Fielding Smith showed the man that beliefs he found strange or objectionable actually had reference in the Bible. Joseph Fielding turned to Luke 7, where Jesus praises John the Baptist's work, to 1 Peter 3, which compares the saving power of baptism to God's salvation of Noah from the flood, and to John 3, where Jesus tells Nicodemus that one must be born again of water and the Holy Spirit to enter into the kingdom of heaven. From these, Fielding Smith insisted that "baptism is essential to my salvation," a point his staunchly Protestant landlord, a believer by salvation in faith alone, denied. In this way, Fielding Smith proved himself a master of an old method of Biblical interpretation, proof-texting, the practice of extracting brief snippets throughout scripture and assembling them to make a broader argument perhaps unrelated to their immediate context.[2]

But the dispute about baptism was embedded in a deeper conceptual argument as well. Alongside his limber use of the Bible, Smith also affirmed that scripture, in the end, could not interpret itself. When Mr. Blood challenged one of Smith's interpretations of a particular biblical text, Smith explained that he believed in this interpretation because it was that of Joseph Smith, which he judged entirely reliable. "God could reveal to man his mind and will today as much as he ever did, and it would be unto us as scripture," Fielding Smith said.[3] It was that insistence that ultimately turned Mr. Blood off from the religion of his young tenant.

Though Fielding Smith lost Mr. Blood, the claim is useful for later interpreters. It illustrated the young Smith's own assumptions about what scripture was and how it was to be used. Despite his insistence to Blood that it was possible to deduce exactly how one needed to be saved—that is, by being baptized—from the text of the Bible read at face value, Fielding Smith also believed that the Bible, or the other scripture he as a Latter-day Saint believed in, was not self-interpreting. It required continuing influence from God to be read properly. And that was why Fielding Smith believed only members of his church rightly understood scripture.

To understand how Joseph Fielding Smith read scripture, it is first important to ask what he meant by the word *scripture*. He offered Mr. Blood a definition—scripture was the mind and will of God revealed to human beings. This definition, though, raises questions about whether scripture is text, or whether it could be oral or visual or something else entirely. He also did not explain to Mr. Blood how one might verify whether something was the will of God.

The concept of scripturalization helps untangle such knots. It suggests that scripture is not necessarily any single text. The special properties faith communities ascribe to one text or another are not inherent in the text. Rather, scripture is the method of human relationship with a text. The authority of a text derives from a community's decision to invest faith in the text and, in turn, the community begins to shape itself in reference to the text. The text becomes authoritative. It becomes scripture.[4]

Scripturalization, then, is the give-and-take by which a community reads a text, ascribes authority to it, selects portions and stories within that text to emphasize, and, finally, reshapes its own norms and rhetoric to meet that authoritative reading of the text. Christians read the Hebrew Bible through the lens of the four gospels, for instance, and see Jesus Christ in Exodus and Genesis while Jews do not. These emphases allow communities to turn seemingly complex and sometimes contradictory bundles of texts into a smooth whole, and to select which rules and norms enunciated in them will govern their lives. That process explains why an evangelical Christian like Mr. Blood and a Latter-day Saint like Joseph Fielding Smith could read the same text and take from it very different understandings of how a Christian is supposed to live.

Fielding Smith came to be, at some level, aware of the process. For him, a correct reading of scripture was alchemy, the distillation of two forces. The first was, of course, a text, a set of words on a page. He assumed this text was designed to be comprehensible, that its meanings would be clear and self-evident.

But the second force, paradoxically, was his surety that comprehensible clarity was present only when one read the text through the lenses of Latter-day Saint belief in authority and prophecy. Fielding Smith thus asserted strict belief in scripture, using words like *literally* and *plain* to describe his allegiance to it—words that many conservative Protestants also used to assert that its meaning was self-evidently clear.[5] But he also asserted that plainness only became clear when seen through the lenses of authoritative interpretation by Latter-day Saint leaders and the guidance of God's Holy Spirit—asserting something like the Roman Catholic belief in the *magisterium*, or the authority of ecclesiastical leaders to interpret texts. Holding two seemingly distinct ideas about scripture seemed no paradox to Fielding Smith. He frankly admitted it.

Fielding Smith did not merely assert that scripture plainly said what he claimed it did. He also claimed that plainness was properly revealed through the ways the leaders of the Church—notably, his father, grandfather, and great-uncle, Joseph Smith Jr.—read scripture. And thus, for him, to read scripture became a boundary marker. Coming to a correct interpretation of any particular passage became for him the process of becoming a genuine and loyal Latter-day Saint. The point here is that scripture never stands on its own. It is always something read within the system of meanings and norms generated in a community. For Fielding Smith, to assert that the meaning of scripture was plain but also mediated by prophecy indicated how he believed his church to work.

Proof-Texting and Rational Scripture

As his debate with Mr. Blood shows, at the time of his mission in England Fielding Smith perceived scripture as a collection of propositions, handily divided into verses, which could be assembled and reassembled in the service of various theological arguments. This practice is often derisively called proof-texting, but it has a long history. It is a sign of Fielding Smith's certainty that scripture was clear and accessible, but it also put him in a lineage of interpretation dating back at least to New Testament writers, who extracted singular verses from the Hebrew Bible to identify Jesus Christ as the promised Messiah. Early Christian writers like the theologian Origen followed the same practice. So did the New England Puritans. Famously, at the Puritan Bible teacher Anne Hutchinson's trial for heresy, her accusers invoked a range of passages to show that women should not act as authorities in a church, while Hutchinson herself invoked a range of passages that showed women teaching.[6]

By the time of Joseph Smith, the practice was well established in American Christianity. Orson Pratt, one of the LDS Church's early apostles and perhaps the most important nineteenth century theologian in the Church, studiously combed the Bible for particular verses that might be read as prophecies of his own movement. For Pratt, God's command to Ezekiel to join together a stick labeled for Judah and another for Joseph was a reference to the Bible and the Book of Mormon, despite surrounding verses describing the sticks as nations. In a September 1872 sermon, he quoted the eighty-fifth Psalm to defend Joseph Smith's story of recovering the Book of Mormon from the hill Cumorah. The psalm declares, "Truth shall spring out of the earth," and Pratt identified this as a prophecy, pointing out that "Forty-five years ago, early this morning, plates resembling gold were taken from the earth."[7]

The habit of proof-texting appealed to the Latter-day Saints because it resonated with the assumptions about the Bible they shared with many Protestant Americans. In his earliest piece of published writing, a short history of his ancestor and Joseph Smith's grandfather Asahel Smith, Fielding Smith noted with approval that "he held aloof from all denominations simply because he could not reconcile their teachings with the Scriptures and his reason." He quoted Asahel as insisting that the "Scriptures" and "sound reason" were "two witnesses that stand by the God of the whole earth."[8]

The idea of the "two books" of revelation and reason—one written in the pages of scripture and the other perceived in the natural world around us—was not Asahel's alone but rather reflected a common way of thinking in the nineteenth-century United States. US Protestants blended together a number of assumptions over the first century of US independence to produce a religion that they believed was commonsensical and easily understood. Among their assumptions was the doctrine of "perspicuity," that God intended the Bible to be comprehensible to any reader. Another was "commonsense realism," a Scottish philosophy affirming that human beings' perceptions of the world were basically reliable. Famously, when confronted with philosopher George Berkeley's wonderings about how we can know whether the ideas, images, sounds, and smells our minds generate from sensory input actually correspond to the real world outside our bodies, the realist Samuel Johnson simply slammed a door and suggested that Berkeley's followers walk right through it. Most US universities in the nineteenth century, dominated by Protestant theology and Scottish philosophy, trained their students to believe that their minds were capable of accurately reading both Scripture and nature alike, ideas that ranged far beyond US campuses in the years before the Civil War.⁹

For instance, Brigham Young, second president of the LDS Church, praised his colleague Heber C. Kimball for his ability to "preach the gospel in a plain familiar manner." While working as a missionary in England, Young remembered, Kimball "would take scripture as he needed it out of his own bible and ask, 'now ain't that so?' the reply would be 'yes.' He would say, 'Now you believe this? You see how plain the Gospel is? Come along now' and he would lead them into the waters of Baptism."¹⁰ The Bible that Kimball and Young—a potter and carpenter by their trades—created through scripturalization was simple and comprehensible.

But, fifty years later, when Joseph Fielding Smith was serving his mission in Great Britain, the Bible had come to seem less clear. By the last decades of the nineteenth century, many Christians felt the Bible to be under siege by academics and scientists, biologists who studied Darwin's theory of evolution and archaeologists and historians who began developing the field of "higher criticism" of the Bible, an attempt to read the Bible in the light of ancient sources and to track its composition as a historical text.

Conservative Protestants, many of them professors at divinity schools on the East Coast of the United States, developed a theology of what came to be called "biblical inerrancy." They insisted the Bible was "without error." They emphasized "the plain implication" of its passages, rejecting the idea that the Bible's authors intended their readers to take stories of miracles or the supernatural as symbolic or metaphorical. Instead, conservative

Protestants embraced a theology of "plenary inspiration," the idea that though the original manuscripts of the Bible are no longer extant, they were directly inspired by God and therefore were infallible. These Protestants made room for simile and metaphor—when Jesus says he wishes to gather the people of Jerusalem like a hen her chicks, he does not mean that he has wings—but, over time, more and more began arguing that God had inspired these writers to the precise words they chose, a doctrine called verbal plenary inspiration.[11]

Of course, to call scripture's meaning "plain" as these men did is simply to assert the power of the word in service of one's preferred interpretations of scripture. Denying that interpretation is interpretation is a way to claim for it the authority that comes with presumably being closest to the text. It is a strategy that many contemporary sociologists and anthropologists who study how believers treat texts have often observed. Saying that a text is "without error" does not actually make it without error; saying that a text should be read "literally" does not make its meaning obvious. Rather, such terms are assertions of authority. They assert that the text is important, special, and reliable. But they also link the text to the concerns and beliefs that any given community already believes is in the text. This is the process of scripturalization, by which a group of believers turn a text into scripture—a source of authority—and in so doing make that scripture binding on them, the symbolic center around which they orient their identities.[12]

Like Protestants, Roman Catholics grappled with these new challenges in the interpretation of scripture. Fielding Smith's older contemporary, Pope Leo XIII (1878–1903), issued a series of papal encyclicals taking on some of the same assertions about scripture that Protestants were wrestling with. He popularized among Roman Catholics the term *magisterium*—the doctrine that the pope, not scholars, has the authority to resolve questions of scriptural interpretation.[13] Just as Protestant strategies elevated the authority of scripture itself in words like *plain* and *literal*, Catholic strategies bound the power of scripture to the authority of the church itself. Fielding Smith's own solution would be evocative of both strategies.

As his life went on, Fielding Smith grew increasingly aware that others, from Mr. Blood on, even if they did share his belief that scripture was plain and clear, somehow did not accept his presumably plain interpretations of it. While serving on his mission in London, Smith began a lifelong practice of reading scripture so thoroughly and intently that he memorized it. In a fit of characteristic hyperbole and self-depreciation, he wrote to his wife Louisa that missionaries are "generally supposed to have learned all that the Bible contains or else they have neglected their duties." He was trying. "I have tried all day to learn a passage of scripture and have not got it yet," he told her. "But I am determined to learn it before I am through. It is the 9, 10 and 11 verses of the second chapter of 1st [Corinthians]." Here Smith associates learning what the Bible contains with memorizing its passages, an association of meaning with a strict, close reading of the text that would persist through his life.[14] It reflected his assumption that simply knowing scripture sufficiently would itself produce meaning.

Early on in his mission, Fielding Smith acted on that assumption. He wrote to Louisa that "I met a lady today who said she had no use for the Mormonites as she did not believe as they did." The woman was deeply uncomfortable with Joseph Smith Jr.'s practice of polygamy, and Fielding Smith, aggravated, insisted that he could defend it with scripture. He told Louisa that "The only way to meet these people is to ask them if they believe the Bible and when they say yes you can soon make them wriggle." But even when Smith had cited enough verses to "silence them with the scriptures," as he put it, the woman still "began to abuse our people." It was the same problem he had faced with Mr. Blood, and it bothered him to no end.[15]

Mr. Blood did not join Smith's church. Neither did the woman bothered by polygamy. Another such group Smith met simply baffled him, and his encounter with them was finally evidence that simply engaging in battles over biblical proof texts was not enough. It was a group he simply called "the Brethren" in his diaries and letters. Most likely it was the Plymouth Brethren, a group of Christians that had been flourishing in the British Isles for a half-century by the time Fielding Smith reached them. The Brethren were heartily suspicious of any priestly hierarchy and instead invested all authority in local congregations, who poured themselves into extensive Bible study to best determine the proper mode of worship and organization. John Nelson Darby, one of the founders of the movement, referred to the Bible as "the authoritative revelation of the will of Christ," containing "elementary and foundation[al] truth."[16]

Later in his life, Fielding Smith would encounter Darby's ideas about the Second Coming of Christ again. But on his mission at the opening of the twentieth century, he found Darby's followers immensely frustrating indeed—more so than Mr. Blood or the woman who scorned polygamy. The reason was he found in them the first people able to go head-to-head with him on Bible citations. "I may be called on at any time to address a congregation of Christians (?) who call themselves the Brethren," he wrote to his wife. "I believe they know more about the Bible than any other of the sects we are among. They are the hardest sect we have met here. They have partly offered us the use of their hall if we would go and talk to them. But they want to question us." He told Louisa that the Brethren made him pray. He had to seek some authority beyond the text. "If we will seek for the Spirit of Truth," he said, "we will be able to do some good."[17]

Late in his life, in a conversation with Richard Poll, an LDS historian who taught at Brigham Young University, Fielding Smith acknowledged the "large number" of Church members, and even other Church leaders, "who do not find it possible to accept all of the doctrines which Brother Smith regards as fundamental." Smith assured Poll that "he did not think they should be excommunicated or barred from teaching."[18] The conversation indicates he had learned a lesson from the Brethren—finding the meaning of scripture was not so simple as simply studying the text. Instead, he would have to find a valid lens for its interpretation.

"Reorganites" and Revelation

The words of the Bible alone, Fielding Smith realized, could not persuade the Brethren that they were incorrect. After he returned home to Utah, brooding on the problem, he found that the issue extended to the Book of Mormon and other scripture that Joseph Smith produced as well. After taking a job at the LDS Church Historian's Office, Fielding Smith was drawn into rhetorical combat with members of the Reorganized Church of Jesus Christ of Latter Day Saints.

In 1905, a Toronto newspaper published a piece by Richard Evans, a counselor in the First Presidency of the Reorganized Church, that derided the LDS Church. Upon reading it, twenty-nine-year-old Fielding Smith bristled. At the request of his father, by then the president of the Church, he dashed off a response and inaugurated a several-month-long struggle.[19] Fielding Smith and Evans traded increasingly aggravated open letters. By 1906, the Reorganized Church had sent several missionaries into Utah, where they gave public speeches and published editorials in various newspapers attacking the LDS Church's history of polygamy. Fielding Smith rose in response. He delivered a public sermon denouncing the Reorganized Church; he wrote responses to editorials; eventually, he published three pamphlets collecting his various writings and Evans's replies.

The points of contention were several. Fielding Smith stood staunchly in defense of "blood atonement." Evans claimed that this was a term Brigham Young had coined after ascending to the leadership of the LDS Church when Joseph Smith died. In Evans's reading, Young wanted to drape his impulse to put apostates to death in theological language. Fielding Smith spurned the claim as mere insult and insisted rather that the idea meant "there are certain sins that man may commit for which the atoning blood of Christ does not avail." Fielding Smith argued that Young meant only that murderers should suffer the death penalty for their crimes. Evans also believed that Brigham Young had begun the practice of plural marriage after Joseph Smith's death. Evans's claim relied on a common, but ahistorical, belief among Joseph Smith's children, who led the Reorganized Church, that their father had not been a polygamist. "No one need blame Joseph any more," Evans declared. "Brigham is the self-confessed channel through which polygamy was given to his people." Fielding Smith, the child and grandchild of polygamists from the Smith family, correctly took strong exception to Evans's proposal. The two also sparred over the nature of God, the LDS practices of temple worship, and whether Brigham Young was Joseph Smith's rightful successor.[20]

But behind whatever particular points of theology or practice the two feuded over, for Fielding Smith the controversy was deeper. It frustrated him to no end that Richard Evans and the other Reorganized leaders claimed to accept the Book of Mormon as scripture, claimed to believe that the revelations of Joseph Smith that each church had compiled into a canonized collection each called the Doctrine and Covenants, and yet could nonetheless reject the ways in which Fielding Smith himself interpreted those texts. It was the same problem he had encountered with the Brethren, as biblically literate as Fielding Smith himself and yet skeptical of his assertions about what the Bible said. "You do not believe in blood atonement," he wrote to Evans. "Is not this the more reason why you should discard the Book of Mormon? Are you not at issue with the teachings not only of that book, but also with those of the Bible on this matter? If so, why not discard the Bible, and while you are about it, the Book of Doctrine and Covenants also?"[21]

To settle the dispute with the Reorganized Church (to, at least, his own satisfaction), Smith made explicit his scripturalization. "The Church has accepted the Bible *as far as it is translated correctly*," Smith insisted, invoking in the italics one of Joseph Smith's Articles of Faith for his church. "Therefore, when it is not translated correctly, we should receive the correct translation when it is given. The Prophet says the Hebrew word *Eloheim* is plural and means Gods, and should have been so translated in the Bible throughout. Is that true?"[22]

To his mind, what Fielding Smith was doing here was demonstrating that, in rejecting LDS views, the Reorganized Church was defying scripture. But that was not all. He linked correct interpretation of scripture to acceptance of Joseph Smith's authority as a prophet and that of the leaders of the LDS Church who followed him. The two went hand-in-hand; one could not have the one without the other. Indeed, Fielding Smith attacked the founders of the Reorganization for denying "the right of Joseph Smith or any other man to be a sole mouthpiece of God to the Church; the plenary inspiration and consequent absolute authority of the Scriptures."[23] That Smith paired scripture and prophecy indicated the evolving nature of his way of thinking about how scripture should be read.

On the one hand, that he invoked "plenary inspiration" indicated his high view of scripture. The phrase "plenary inspiration" was popular among American Reformed Protestants, such as those conservative theologians who defended the Bible from higher criticism. Reformed Protestants descended from John Calvin's wing of the Reformation and put particular emphasis on correct doctrine and theology. For them, "plenary inspiration" meant that scripture was without error, that everything in it was relevant to human salvation, and that it was inspired in its language as well as in its ideas. As Benjamin Warfield, a Presbyterian theologian at Princeton Theological Seminary put it in an 1895 essay, "the doctrine of the plenary inspiration of the Scriptures, which looks upon them as an oracular book, in all its parts and elements, alike of God, trustworthy in all its affirmations of every kind, remains today as it has always been, the vital faith of the people of God, and the formal teaching of the organized Church."[24] Fielding Smith was demonstrating that he was conversant in the language of conservative Protestantism for defending the authority of scripture.

And yet, as his experiences in England had proven to Fielding Smith, he was no Protestant. Though he might invoke a Protestant doctrine of scripture, what he claimed it to say would never please Protestants like

Mr. Blood. Because of that, he was becoming aware that scripture should not simply be read; it had to be read correctly. When it was read correctly, it was obvious what it said; when it was read incorrectly, it was obviously misread. And for Fielding Smith, it was correctly read through the guidance of a priestly and prophetic caste.

In the late 1940s, Fielding Smith explained all this to his son Douglas, who was serving a mission in the Pacific Northwest, roaming from Seattle to Yakima to even Alaska. In January 1949, Douglas wrote to his father frustrated. He had been presenting people with copies of the Book of Mormon, asking them to read it, and yet they seemed unimpressed. Fielding Smith explained why with an example. "We accept, for instance, the doctrine of the resurrection," he pointed out. "Of course we can turn to the scriptures and show that the prophets have spoken of this doctrine." He and Douglas could even point to the witnesses who had seen Christ raised. "The trouble is," Fielding Smith explained, "most men do not follow the guidance of the Spirit which is given them and therefore they do not come to the truth."[25]

Fielding Smith also disseminated the idea in his writings for the Church more broadly. "I suppose there is no passage of scripture that has caused more controversy, that has been called in question more, that has been less understood than this passage in the last chapter of Malachi. It took a revelation from God in this age in which we live to make known what it means," he wrote once, referring to a revelation dictated by his ancestor Joseph Smith that, as far as Fielding Smith was concerned, settled the question of what a passage in the Hebrew prophet Malachi meant.[26]

The Standard Works

Fielding Smith's belief in a Mormon form of scripturalization helps to explain his beliefs about the Book of Mormon and, more, why it was that the Church of Jesus Christ of Latter-day Saints claimed four volumes of scripture rather than a single Bible.

Fielding Smith believed it was important to make distinctions among the four volumes. Indeed, he was willing to, after a fashion, rank them. "In my judgment there is no book on earth yet come to man as important as the book known as the Doctrine and Covenants, with all due respect to the Book of Mormon, and the Bible, and the Pearl of Great Price, which we say are our standards in doctrine," he said. His reason was that those three texts were "doctrine and commandments given to the people anciently." The Doctrine and Covenants, on the other hand, a collection of revelations dictated by Joseph Smith, "is our book. It belongs to the Latter-day Saints."[27]

The distinction was significant to him. Fielding Smith believed that the interplay between the written texts themselves and particular leaders in particular offices and inspired by God in particular times and places in history was what made scripture scripture. Scripture was intended to convey certain messages to certain people at certain times and would be best understood by the people for whom it was intended. He also believed such relationships existed among various volumes of scripture as well. They clarified each other, filled each other's gaps, and stood as witnesses to each other. To do this they had to be different yet also mutually related, balancing each other and answering each other's questions. These beliefs bring to mind the anthropologist Brian Malley's notion of the "relevance" of scripture. For Malley, a student of contemporary evangelicals in the United States, a significant part of what evangelical Christians mean when they say that scripture is to be taken literally or without error is that scripture is relevant and important, not obscure or extraneous. For Fielding Smith, multiple volumes of scripture were tools for reading each other but also for asserting that each volume was relevant in a particular way.[28]

Fielding Smith placed a great deal of weight on what he called "the divine law of witnesses." Citing the apostle Paul's statement that "In the mouth of two or three witnesses shall every word be established," Fielding Smith claimed that "This law the Lord has always followed in granting new revelation." He explained that Noah did not preach alone; that Moses had allies; that both Jesus and Joseph Smith called twelve apostles. And, he claimed, scriptures served as witnesses to each other. Literary critics might call this idea intertextuality—how texts refer to, relate to, and interpret each other.[29]

He once levied the point in a debate with J. Reuben Clark, a member of the Church's First Presidency, who in a 1946 speech used the word *mortal* to describe the bodies of Adam and Eve. Fielding Smith objected. "When the earth was created it was not given a 'mortal creation' but a physical creation," he informed Clark, urging him to use the latter word in the future. Fielding Smith understood scripture to say there had been no death before the fall of Adam and Eve. To justify his argument, Fielding Smith declared that "The account of the creation of the Earth as is given in Genesis, the

Book of Moses, the Book of Abraham and as given in the Temple, is the creation of the physical earth, and of physical animals and plants. I think the Temple account, which we understand was given by revelation, is the clearest of all of these." Throughout the letter, he compared various discussions of the creation in all these texts and the Book of Mormon to arrive at his conclusion. For Fielding Smith, the various accounts of creation given in Genesis and Joseph Smith's books of Moses and Abraham and the ritual endowment ceremony in LDS temples were not to be understood as distinct or perhaps contradictory accounts, but as interlocking and mutually clarifying.[30]

This was consistent with how Fielding Smith approached scripture throughout his life. "We will cling to the Bible because we know that whatever errors there are, they are the errors of uninspired men who have done the translating," he said. Unlike the Bible, "the Book of Mormon comes to us pure, having been translated by divine power, and it contains incontrovertible internal evidence to those who read it and know anything about the power and Spirit of God. . . . besides which we have the Doctrine and Covenants, and these three witnesses enable us to occupy a different position from any other religious denomination upon the face of the earth." Each book of scripture was to be read in a somewhat different way, each book had different intentions, each book different strengths; but, lined up together, they were witnesses of each other.[31]

Citing this rule, Fielding Smith said, "Guided by the Book of Mormon, Doctrine and Covenants, and the Spirit of the Lord, it is not difficult for one to discern the errors in the Bible." This was not to say that the Bible was useless, but Fielding Smith believed God allowed it to have errors so that other books of scripture could correct them, thus validating each other through the proof of their evident relationship.[32]

Just so, those other books depended on the Bible as well. "There also must be some inspired utterances in the Bible bearing witness to the Book of Mormon," Fielding Smith claimed. "If there were no such references, there would be a serious defect in the testimony of the record of the Nephites." If the Book of Mormon lacked witnesses, its status as scripture could be doubted. Joseph Smith showed the plates from which he translated the book to witnesses for this reason, but, according to Fielding Smith, the Bible also testified of the Book of Mormon. He charted passages in Isaiah and the Gospel of John as allusions to the book. He also claimed that Joseph Smith himself was a living embodiment of intertextuality. The blessing of

Jacob on his son Joseph of Egypt at the end of the Book of Genesis was, according to Fielding Smith, a prophecy of the Book of Mormon. Joseph's descendants were "to inherit a land far from Jerusalem and become a multitude of nations." Fielding Smith understood this place to be the Americas, colonized originally by the descendants of Joseph through his son Ephraim described in the Book of Mormon. And then, of course, Joseph Smith himself emerged, according to Fielding Smith and the Book of Mormon itself descended from Joseph in Egypt, "a pure Ephraimite," who stood as translator of the Book of Mormon in order to witness to it by his word and his existence alike. For Fielding Smith, the great cycle of witness, authority, and scripturalization flowed through itself and back again, and nowhere more evidently than in the Book of Mormon.[33]

This way of understanding the meaning of the Book of Mormon through intertextual prophecies and relationships was one reason that Fielding Smith was relatively uninterested in debates about archaeology and Book of Mormon evidences, the sort of thing that fascinated other intellectually inclined Church leaders of his generation. The beginning of the twentieth century was the great age of what some scholars call "biblical archaeology," an Anglo-American school of amateurs and professionals passionate about locating archaeological evidence for biblical narratives in Palestine, Egypt, and elsewhere in the Middle East. British and American archaeologists, trained and not, flooded Jerusalem and Egypt and claimed to have located a host of sites, from Jesus's true tomb to the walls of the biblical city of Jericho.[34] Many LDS scholars believed the same thing could be done with the Book of Mormon and archaeology in Mesoamerica. "Every new discovery in American archaeology tends to confirm the truth of the Book of Mormon," the apostle John Widtsoe declared in a General Conference of the Church, citing discoveries in the Mayan ruins.[35]

Fielding Smith followed such affairs with mild interest and tended to assume that archaeology would obviously demonstrate the historicity of the Book of Mormon. (Occasionally he would point to, for instance, the ruins of ancient copper mines in the Americas.[36]) But he preferred instead to invoke the prophetic and intertextual meanings the texts offered as proof of their divinity. As he said in one talk on the Book of Mormon, "If this book were merely a history of that people as Dickens' 'History,' or Fiske's 'History' is of America, it would not be so important." What interested Fielding Smith was not the book's relationship with material evidence. Instead he invoked prophetic proofs for the book. "People sometimes ask the question, 'Why is it that if Joseph Smith had the plates, that he did not keep them,'" Fielding Smith said. But "The Lord tries the faith of his people. He gives them witnesses in his own way." Fielding Smith cited the witness of Joseph Smith and his associates; he invoked biblical prophecy he claimed referred to the Book of Mormon.[37]

In 1937, Albert Hunter, a skeptical academic, wrote to Fielding Smith asking for tangible proof of the Book of Mormon's historicity. Fielding Smith, with a nearly audible sigh, referred him to books by Latter-day Saints J. M. Sjodahl and John Widtsoe, who offered reams of archaeological parallels. But he opened his letter with a long paragraph that culminated with this: "The best that archaeology can do is to bear witness to the historical setting; it will not prove the writings to be the word of God." He urged Hunter to study the New Testament and the statements of the witnesses to the Book of Mormon printed in the introduction to that text. He cited intertextual evidence in the Bible and the Doctrine and Covenants. He then assured Hunter that he must "follow the formula given by the Lord if you wish to know of his doctrine."[38]

This set of relationships among the various books of scripture shows the close connections Joseph Fielding Smith drew between texts and communities, people and books as he determined who held authority and why in the Church of Jesus Christ of Latter-day Saints. They also illustrate that scripture was not simply text to him; it was rather a nexus of influences, knowledge, and relationships.

The Warfare between Science and Religion

By the time Fielding Smith settled into his seventies—old age for most, but for such a long-lived man, merely his maturity—he had become the dominant theological voice in the Church. He was by then clear about the deep interconnections between text and the inspiration of the Church's leaders. In the Church's 1950 General Conference, he asked, "Do the people of the world know where they are going when they die? No. They sing about a beautiful isle of somewhere. They do not know. Can they find out in the Bible? Yes, we can find it. They could find it if they had the right inspiration. But with the added help that we obtain from the records the Lord has given us, we do not stumble over that."[39]

Fielding Smith's magnum opus, *Man: His Origin and Destiny,* was published a few years later, in 1954. In it, he not only laid out the sort of authority he ascribed to scripture. He also crystallized an idea that had been developing in him since his youthful arguments with Richard Evans and Mr. Blood. He became increasingly convinced that the route to clear scriptural interpretation was so obvious that those who rejected it were acting in bad faith.

"The misinterpretations of the scriptures, the mistakes that crept into them, or were deliberately placed there by scribes and priests who did not understand the truth, cannot be blamed upon the original writers," he claimed. And such conscious manipulation of the texts continued. Fielding Smith described two contemporary camps of critics who he believed were destroying proper scriptural interpretation. The first were "higher critics," those who, according to Fielding Smith, "proclaim that the books of the Bible are without divine inspiration and were not written at the time indicated by the record." The second were those interested in "the geological history of the Earth." Both were "bent upon the destruction of the story of creation and the development of humanity as this story is told in the Bible."[40]

Fielding Smith found a foil who to him represented both in a British-born Latter-day Saint named B. H. Roberts.

By the early twentieth century, Brigham Henry Roberts, a president of the Quorum of the Seventy, the third tier of leaders in the Church, was growing increasingly preoccupied with the higher criticism of the Bible. A generation older than Fielding Smith, Roberts had a reputation as perhaps the most vociferous and sharp-tongued defender of the Church in his day, a reputation that one might think would have made him an ally of the like-minded Fielding Smith. Indeed, Roberts worked part-time under Smith in the Church Historian's Office.

And yet, by the 1920s, the decade Fielding Smith turned fifty and Roberts entered his seventies, the two men had come into conflict. The causes were several. Both, their colleagues admitted, had irascible and strong-willed personalities. Neither suffered fools well, and both, at times, made that judgment of the other. Roberts was sympathetic to the Democratic Party, Smith to the Republicans. In October 1928, Roberts delivered a speech defending Governor Al Smith of New York, the Democratic nominee for president; Fielding Smith saved a copy of a newspaper report and noted at the top, "A very unwise speech by a very unwise man."[41]

But beyond issues of partisanship and personality, the clash had real intellectual heft to it. Both men were autodidacts; neither had much formal education. But while Roberts worked hard to familiarize himself with contemporary scholarship, respected those who produced it, and wanted to participate in its conversations, Smith had little but scorn for most professional scholars. Roberts believed that such work could enrich his religious faith—one reason why many scholars that have followed have taken Roberts's side in these disputes—while Smith viewed scholarship as destructive of faith. It was these disagreements that fueled the clash.

When he first encountered geology and the higher criticism, Roberts was skeptical. But at some point in the early twentieth century, he read Charles Elliott's *The Mosaic Authorship of the Pentateuch,* an 1884 study that attempted to defend the notion that Moses authored the first five books of the Hebrew Bible, and was impressed. Elliott urged respect for the higher criticism's techniques. By the time he delivered a speech in Logan, Utah, in 1911, Roberts was counseling Latter-day Saints to consider that "The methods, then, of higher criticism we recognize as proper; but we must disagree as to the correctness of many of the conclusions arrived at by that method." As did Elliott, Roberts defended the Mosaic authorship of the book of Genesis; he rejected the conclusion of many higher critics that the book of Isaiah was a composite text of multiple authors. But he also insisted that the higher criticism rightly understood "merely attacks an apostate Christianity's misconceptions and false interpretations of the Bible." He was sure such attentive analysis of scripture would ultimately validate his faith.[42]

Fielding Smith didn't believe it.

In contradistinction to Roberts's willingness to integrate the tools of scholarship with his religious faith, Fielding Smith adapted an increasingly popular narrative advanced by a number of writers as the nineteenth century ended. The narrative posited that science and religion were essentially, and inevitably, at war. John William Draper was a chemist and for a time president of New York University; Andrew Dickson White was a historian and president of Cornell University. The titles of their books—*History of the Conflict between Religion and Science* and *A History of the Warfare of Science with Theology in Christendom,* respectively—give some sense of their argument.[43]

For centuries, the idea of science in the Christian world had been intimately intertwined with religion. Many scientists during the previous few hundred years of European history had understood the two concepts as aspects of each other, the sort of idea that gave life to Asahel Smith's notion of the twin revelations of God in revelation and reason. But White and

Draper told a different story. For them, religion and science were fundamentally different ways of knowing. They saw the steady advance of the latter occurring at the expense of the former. Science relied on reason, religion on authority. As Draper explained, human history was a "narrative of the conflict of two contending powers, the expansive force of the human intellect on one side, and the compression arising from traditionary faith and human interests on the other." The simplified, ahistorical morality tales White and Draper told—of Galileo's struggle with the Roman Catholic Church, of Charles Darwin's abandonment of his faith—were repeated for decades and served the easy dichotomies of their narrative.[44]

Draper and White hoped their stories would eliminate the sort of religion they believed dogmatically strangled scholarship in its crib. But Fielding Smith read their work too. Smith embraced the conflict thesis, but the side he took would have surprised the two college presidents. While they intended to celebrate the rise of science in the face of traditional authority, for Fielding Smith, reason and authority properly understood went hand-in-hand. The false authorities of science flew in the face both of reason and of revelation.

"Mr. Charles Darwin was first trained for the ministry. He accepted belief in God. After making his research and reaching his deductions, he forsook belief in God," Fielding Smith reported, repeating the story that White and Draper told. Then Fielding Smith turned the story on the conflict theorists themselves. "So it has been with the many scores of others. They had to renounce their faith in the atonement of Jesus Christ, for they rejected their faith in the fall of Adam. So it was with Dr. Andrew D. White, who became a bitter opponent of the fall and atonement. Their theories are not compatible with faith in the God of the scriptures."[45]

Fielding Smith grew only increasingly sure that such figures as Darwin and White had purposefully, intentionally chosen to turn away from revelation, and his deep suspicion of the corrosive effects of science is characteristically antimodern. Through the 1920s and 1930s, he began to seek out other antimoderns who read scripture as he did, even those outside the LDS Church, and credited them with holding more closely to his twin metrics of plain reading of scripture and adherence to the authority of revelation than did skeptics within the church. He maintained a cordial correspondence with George McCready Price, a Seventh-day Adventist and perhaps the most prominent advocate of creationism in the United States

36

at the time, telling Price "What you have written appeals to me. It seems to be far more reasonable, and I know it is in accord with divine revelation. This I can not say for the orthodox view on geology."[46]

Thus, when Brigham Henry Roberts began his work of rapprochement between traditional LDS belief and the findings of the higher criticism, Fielding Smith was predisposed to be skeptical. As he watched Roberts work, he did so with a sharp eye for the process he believed inevitable: as Roberts began to accept the conclusions of scholarship, he would lose the influence of divine revelation and would invariably began to interpret scripture incorrectly.

The Age of the Earth

Though Joseph Fielding Smith despised the higher criticism, at least he read something of it. In April 1930, he gave a speech to the Genealogical Society of Utah, a Church-founded organization that he led, in which he explained some of the basic theories of contemporary higher critics in order to debunk them with inspiration. He attacked those who claimed that the story of creation in Genesis 1–3 contained the work of "at least two different writers in different periods." And yet, not only were modern scholars mistaken, but so were those who wanted "to square the teachings in the Bible with the teachings of modern science and philosophy with regard to the age of the earth and life upon it." He did not name names, but he did archly note that "even in the Church there are a scattered few" who believed, wrote, and taught that the Earth might well be billions of years old, and that many species and lives might have lived or died before God placed Adam and Eve in the Garden of Eden. This, Fielding Smith said, ran counter to "the doctrine which has been taught by authority in the Church regarding Adam."[47]

Fielding Smith was referring here to Roberts. Two years earlier Rudger Clawson, president of the Quorum of the Twelve Apostles, had appointed Fielding Smith to a committee of five apostles responsible for reviewing Roberts's new manuscript, "The Truth, The Way, The Life," a massive comprehensive theology that Roberts intended to be the final statement of his life's work on the history and philosophy of religion. Upon reading it, Fielding Smith had discovered Roberts endorsed an ancient earth, hundreds of millions years old, and cited a great deal of archaeological evidence for ancient hominids, whom he speculated lived before God had planted Adam and Eve upon the earth. That was why in the King James Version's text of Genesis 3 God instructed the two to "replenish" (which Roberts took to mean "refill") the earth. The reports the committee returned to Clawson and the First Presidency were mixed, particularly with reference to Roberts's speculations.[48]

By 1930, Fielding Smith felt comfortable referring to Roberts's work, if not his name, in public. In castigating Roberts, Fielding Smith appealed not only to what seemed to him the plain reading of scripture, but also to the authority of the Church in interpreting what scripture said. Of course, Fielding Smith's appeal to church authority did not mean that church authority was unified on the question. Many, including Fielding Smith's own colleagues as apostles James E. Talmage and John A. Widstoe, were sympathetic to Roberts on the question of the age of the earth. But the most important authorities to Fielding Smith were his own family: his great uncle Joseph Smith, church founder, and his father, Joseph F. Smith. "If we accept the revelations which have come through the prophet Joseph Smith we know that the teachings of the modern scholars in this regard are not true," he said.[49]

In Fielding Smith's mind, next to them, where could B. H. Roberts stand?

But Roberts tried. He saw precisely what Fielding Smith was doing and sought to counter each of the younger man's assumptions about scripture. In December 1930, he wrote to Church president Heber J. Grant and questioned whether Fielding Smith's arguments should be taken as the official position of the Church. If not, Roberts said, Fielding Smith was "in conflict with the plain implication at least of the scriptures" but also with "the teaching of a more experienced, learned and earlier Apostle than himself." Here Roberts meant Orson Hyde, president of the Quorum of the Twelve Apostles under Brigham Young, who had believed there was life and death on the earth before Adam and Eve.[50]

Roberts sought not only to argue that Fielding Smith was incorrect in his assumptions about the age of the earth and the existence of life before Adam and Eve but also to demonstrate that Fielding Smith's assumptions about the nature of scripture were incorrect—first, that the scriptures could sustain a single plain reading and, second, that such a single plain reading could be validated by appeals to the authority of Church leaders. Throughout "The Truth, the Way, the Life," Roberts spoke of scripture as a text that could be subject to multiple interpretations, that might lack clarity—and not simply a lack of clarity to be easily illuminated through revelation, but the sort of lack of clarity that might lead to multiple plausible interpretations. "Christianity set forth in the New Testament, I know, is supposed to have furnished revealed knowledge concerning these things. But does it?" Roberts asked wryly, implying troubling questions about human nature, existence, and preexistence. He worried that it did not and such troubling questions were not limited to the Bible alone. Roberts commented elsewhere about Joseph Smith's revelations in the Books of Moses and Abraham, noting that "It may be admitted that there is some lack of clearness in what is revealed, owing to the fragmentary character of the book of Abraham, and only the partial interpretation that our prophet gives of it." Finally, he was willing to look to sources outside scripture and revelation to explain what those things might mean. "What science discovers helps us to realize the greatness and wonderfulness of this revelation," he said of Joseph Smith's new scriptures.[51]

The night before New Year's Eve 1930, Roberts had a telephone conversation with Rudger Clawson, the president of the Quorum of the Twelve Apostles, in which he tried to lay out these ideas and explain why he found Fielding Smith's critiques so troubling. He argued that the narrative of conflict between science and religion that Fielding Smith promoted was misleading. He insisted that, in fact, by rejecting any tool for interpretation beyond the authority of Church leaders, Fielding Smith was misunderstanding scriptures, which required a multiplicity of tools to understand correctly. Fielding Smith's position was "contrary to a great deal of well developed and ascertained truth established by the researches of scientists of the highest character," Roberts said. "I hold his doctrine contrary at least to the plain implications of the scriptures."[52] Labeling scripture "plain" was, it became obvious, an attempt on each man's part to assert the authority of clarity for his own position.

Clawson and other members of the Quorum of the Twelve were torn between two intractable and intelligent men. The committee assigned to read Roberts's work was generally unsympathetic to his speculations. But that hardly meant they were willing to subscribe to Fielding Smith's.[53]

They asked both men to submit defenses of their positions, and Fielding Smith's sixty-four-page broadside was a full-throated explication of his twin opinions that the scriptures were obvious on the points he claimed them to be and that their obviousness was understood and explicated only through the line of church authority that led back to his great-uncle Joseph Smith.

Fielding Smith's position was evident in his concluding statement, in which he managed to assert scriptural authority, a sort of Mormon magisterium, and his own familial ties to the latter. "With this great array before me of revelation and Scriptural interpretation by the leading authorities of the Church from the beginning and having imbibed this doctrine from contact with some of them," he declared, "and from my study of the Scriptures, I certainly feel that I have both the authority and the justification to speak with emphasis." He drove the point home again. "If I am wrong, then the revelations are wrong—I have not placed private interpretation upon them—but the same interpretation that the leading elders of the Church have placed upon them, including the Prophet Joseph Smith."[54]

Fielding Smith insisted throughout his life he was not in opposition to all science—merely science that did not understand its place beneath revelation. "Knowledge and intelligence are not synonymous terms," he explained in 1937 to the Church's two commissioners of education. "Why did the Lord choose the unlearned boy Joseph Smith rather than one of these great scholars?" he asked. It was because modern scholars believed the Bible to be full of "superstitious scribes and uninspired prophets." Joseph Smith, on the other hand, in his ostensible naïveté, trusted revelation rather than scholarship.[55]

Unresolved Tension

Neither Roberts nor Fielding Smith prevailed in their contest. Although most other church leaders seemed somewhat more skeptical of Roberts's speculations than of Fielding Smith's attempts at rigorous adherence to text, ultimately the Church's First Presidency resolved that it cared more about preserving the perception of unity among the Church's leadership than about clarifying the precise details of the creation. As president of the Church Heber J. Grant wrote in his diary, "the controversy over whether the earth was inhabited before Adam should be left alone; no good comes from dealing in mysteries." But in so doing, the First Presidency implicitly gently reframed Fielding Smith's position as much as it did that of Roberts, whose book would remain unpublished. "Neither side of the controversy has been accepted as doctrine," the First Presidency wrote. "Leave geology, biology, archaeology and anthropology, no one of which has to do with the salvation of the souls of mankind, to scientific research."[56]

The question of the creation of the earth aside, the First Presidency here took a position on method. It adopted Fielding Smith's position that science and religion were distinct things, subtly rejecting Roberts's insistence that the two fields of knowledge might inform each other. But, at the same time, it also declined to adopt Fielding Smith's position that scriptural questions could be answered with absolute clarity or that the interpretation of earlier church leaders might be accepted as authoritative. Fielding Smith regularly found other Church leaders unwilling to adopt his views wholesale. But most, like the First Presidency, were unwilling to take him on in open debate. There, Roberts was an outlier. For instance, upon receiving Fielding Smith's corrections about his use of the term *mortal*, the generally pugnacious J. Reuben Clark wrote back, "You seem to think I reject the scriptures," he said. "I do not intend to do so but obviously I am no more bound by your interpretation of them than you are by mine." The difference, Clark stated, was this: "You do not accept the scriptural record as given in historical sequence; I do." As with Roberts, he showed Fielding Smith that the notion that scripture was plain and clear could cut both ways.[57]

And yet, Clark said, "I shall make such adjustments in the text as will, I hope, let us by one another without the necessity of a public disagreement." He omitted *mortal* from the published version of the talk.[58]

In his refutation of Roberts, Fielding Smith wrote, "So called 'science' has, changed from age to age in its deductions, and as divine revelation is truth, and must abide forever, views as to the lesser should conform to the positive statements of the former."[59] This was why, in the end, Fielding Smith could celebrate both his ancestor Asahel Smith's embrace of reason and revelation both and at the same time commit himself to a theory of conflict between science and religion. Just as various works of scripture and various interpreters thereof should find their place in a great network of hierarchy and relationship that facilitated proper understanding of the world, so should science take its real place subordinate to scripture and in so doing find its real purpose. Scripture, for him, was relevant not simply to text, but to the entire web of human knowledge and relationships in the world.

CHAPTER THREE

Progress

In April 1962, Joseph Fielding Smith visited Tulsa, Oklahoma. He was there in his capacity as president of the Quorum of the Twelve Apostles, attending a local church conference and visiting with Oklahomans who were not members of the Church but curious about it. He met with a reporter, who, offhandedly, asked the eighty-five-year-old Church leader about travel to the moon.

The moon was on people's minds. President John F. Kennedy had been in office for just over a year by that point. He had already made a moon landing a priority. In April 1961, the Soviet Union had successfully sent the first human being into space. The next month, Kennedy, hoping to regain the US initiative, convened a joint session of Congress and told them he wanted the United States to send a man to the moon and bring him home again before the end of the decade. Congress devoted vast resources to what came to be known as the Apollo Program and, by 1962, the space race with the Soviet Union was regularly making the news and thrilling US citizens.[1]

It surprised the reporter, then, when Fielding Smith threw cold water on the whole idea. "Man does not belong on the moon," he said shortly, assuring the reporter that he "based his belief on his interpretation of the scriptures." The story was picked up by press wires and reprinted all over the country, bringing Fielding Smith a bit of grief. "I am flooded by letters in relation to it," he complained to his journal, "with some editorial criticism. Why such a fuss?"[2]

And yet it was not in Fielding Smith's nature to back down. On May 1, 1962, he sent a letter to Robert Echols, a teacher in the Church's education system. He told Echols that he was not responding to the vast number of letters he had received about the moon but would make an exception for

Echols "because of the importance of the answer to you and the boys and girls in the seminary system."

Then he explained to Echols why he had made the point. "The moon is of a higher order than the earth according to the reckoning of the Lord," he said. And he went on: "We were placed here as prisoners, so to speak, at least confined to mortality for a reason, to be tried and proved to be worth of an exaltation or some other condition in the life to come." His concluding thoughts did not give an inch. He wrote to Echols, "It is my judgment that Earth-men who are mortal have no place on the moon or to have anything to do with the moon."[3]

Far from being simply an antiscientific crank, Fielding Smith offered a coherent vision of the nature of human history, one that deviated starkly from that of many other early-twentieth-century Americans. To put it simply, Joseph Fielding Smith did not believe in progress.

In 1954, Fielding Smith published his masterwork *Man: His Origin and Destiny*, a sweeping defense of the story of humanity as told in scripture. He spent pages upon pages refuting the theory of evolution and defending the historical reality of the Garden of Eden. He expended so much effort that the broader structures behind those arguments are easy to miss. Fielding Smith believed a strict reading of scripture required him to reject the theory of evolution as a principle of biology. But he also rejected evolution as a principle of history. Put another way, not only did he deny the idea that human beings were the product of a long process of biological development; he denied also the idea that human cultures and civilizations were likewise the product of centuries of historical development.

Among the more important of Fielding Smith's conclusions is buried toward the end of the book. In a discussion of the fall of Adam and Eve, he observes that, after the first humans left the Garden of Eden, "the earth became suited to Adam's condition and became a temporal earth, or subject to all the conditions of morality and death." Just so, Fielding Smith promised that the earth itself, like the human beings on it, "will die and receive its resurrection."[4]

In an exchange with the LDS scientist Henry Eyring, who had written Fielding Smith to protest his attacks on the theory of evolution, Fielding Smith explained that the earth, and all earths, would pass through four states: the "creation, and condition antedating the fall; 2) the telestial condition which has prevailed since the fall of Adam; 3) the renewal, or restoration, which has commenced since the restoration of the Gospel[;] ... 4) the celestial, or final state of the earth when it has obtained its exaltation." There were, Fielding Smith said, millions upon millions of earths, each populated in turn, shepherding human beings through the cycles of their own progress and participating in the rhythms of creation, fall, and restoration themselves.[5]

The belief arose from fundamental principles in Joseph Fielding Smith's conception of order in the universe. For him, the gestalt of the universe was not linear, it was cyclical. From pieces as small as the individual human life to as large as the very earth itself, Fielding Smith expected the same pattern, and he thought it not merely foolish but impossible for human beings, in their own lives or as a society, to attempt to defy it. That was why he did not believe a man would ever land on the moon.

The Laws of History

Joseph Fielding Smith grew up in a society that believed in civilization. As Europeans expanded their military power, the authority of Christianity, and European economic, domestic, and cultural norms across the globe in the eighteenth and nineteenth centuries, they also began to explain why such a thing was good and necessary. One of the reasons was the concept of "civilization," a word first used perhaps surprisingly late. Its initial appearance in English was in 1772, a few years after it was coined in French.[6]

By the 1820s, the French historian Francois Guizot could suggest that "There is, in reality, a general destiny of humanity, a transmission of the aggregate of civilization" and "the idea of progress, of development, appears to me the fundamental idea contained in the world civilization."[7] Guizot took for granted that there was something called "civilization" in the first place; that it was a coherent concept that aggregated various aspects of human society—economy, family life, religion, politics, art—into a whole that illuminated some sort of essential identity. After him, writer after writer in the nineteenth century took stabs at systematizing the various components of civilization, showing how they related to each other. Almost immediately, Western writers from Thomas Jefferson to Karl Marx took the idea for granted and suggested that not only did civilizations exist—they had identifiable teleologies. Civilizations rose and fell. Their lives moved in linear fashion. They progressed.[8]

Even before Charles Darwin, theories of civilization were steeped in evo-lutionary ideas, particularly those of Jean-Baptiste Lamarck, an eighteenth-century French theorist who suggested that species passed on acquired, rather than inherited, traits. As early as Lamarck, social philosophers had seized on the concept of evolution to suggest that it described not merely biology but also society. Civilizations, Lamarckian theorists argued, would improve or fail in accord with the values and behaviors of its members. To use the phrase coined by the popular Lamarckian theorist Herbert Spencer, survival of the fittest explained not merely how species might evolve over time, but also why. Spencer argued that just as "the savage has taken the place of the lower creatures, so must he, if he remained too long a savage, give place to his superior."[9] For Spencer, civilization evolved from the simple state of savagery to the complicated world of law and culture.

Writers like the American Lewis Morgan followed Spencer, plotting out stages of civilization from savagery to barbarism, to, inevitably, modern, democratic, capitalist, Protestant societies.[10] E. B. Tylor, one of the founders of religious studies, observed that his own work relied on that of Spencer and Morgan. He theorized that religion also evolved hand-in-hand with other signifiers of civilization, from apparently primitive animism, in which human beings sought to appease spiritual beings associated with the physi-cal world, to modern ethical religion, which rejected irrational beliefs in favor of positive moral discipline.[11] Other theorists, like the French anthro-pologist Arthur de Gobineau, linked civilization to race. He argued that a civilization required both abstract and practical virtues and believed that it was possible to create "civilization only in races which possess, in high degree, either of the two without being too much deficit in the other."[12] Gobineau repeated ideas about struggle, survival, and progress that were similar to those Spencer and others drew from Darwin.

The concept of civilization and its relationship to questions of race, religion, government, gender, and half a hundred more particular factors became increasingly important to Americans by the early twentieth cen-tury. Most took the idea of progress for granted and linked it to moral and material success. "Progress there must and shall be," declared Theodore Roosevelt in 1910. "Our past century has been one of gigantic material prosperity. . . . [I]t is a great good chiefly as a means for the upbuilding upon it of a high and fine type of character."[13]

Progress was invoked in debates over education, immigration, the increasingly powerful Jim Crow regime in the South, and the expanding influence of US imperialism abroad. Latter-day Saints were not excepted. The idea of civilization was invoked in debates over Book of Mormon historicity, in conversations about how the Latter-day Saints were to become participants in US politics and society after the end of plural marriage, in discussions about what it meant to build Zion.

And while most Latter-day Saint leaders adopted some form of these conventional ideas about civilization and progress, Joseph Fielding Smith forged his own way. He looked at them all and saw a basic assumption he found objectionable: the notion that, over time, humans and their history changed.

The History of the Church

In 1922, two years after Fielding Smith asked fellow apostle David O. McKay to advocate for the project before the president of the Church, his book *Essentials in Church History* was published by the Deseret News Press, which is owned by the Church.[14] The volume consolidated a number of ideas about the nature of history that other Church intellectuals like Talmage and B. H. Roberts had already offered in similar histories of the Church, but also extended them, offering a systematic way of thinking about how history worked that Fielding Smith would go on to repeat throughout his life.

The theory of history that Joseph Fielding Smith posits in the book was not that of trained historians. Over the course of Fielding Smith's life, the practice of history professionalized in Germany, the United Kingdom, and the United States. Professional historians learned to privilege documents and evidence, and to discount claims that could not be supported with citations and archival research. In his work, Fielding Smith rejected this means of doing history.[15] Rather, he preferred to anchor knowledge about the past in what sacred texts claimed about how history functioned. In this, Fielding Smith was like Jonathan Edwards, the great Puritan theologian and historian. Edwards argued that the history of the Bible "alone gives us an account of the first original of all things, and this history alone deduces things down in a wonderful series from the original, giving an idea of the grand scheme of divine providence as tending to its great end."[16] Like

Edwards, Fielding Smith believed that, before one could understand history, one must understand the divine laws that governed it. History should be measured against scripture.

Fielding Smith began his history of the LDS church with human history as told in the Bible. Talmage began his book with the premortal existence of the human race as told in LDS scripture and with the creation of the world as told in Genesis. B. H. Roberts introduced his six-volume history of the church with Jesus Christ's life. Both Roberts and Fielding Smith began with an assertion that, as Roberts put it, "the Gospel of Jesus Christ has existed from the very earliest ages of the world."[17] Fielding Smith phrased it only slightly differently: "The Gospel is much older than the law of Moses; it existed before the foundation of the world."[18] All these LDS historians, then, positioned the story of human history as the story of their own religion.

And yet there were subtle distinctions between the men. Roberts drew on the long-standing Christian idea of dispensations, adapting it in the same way that many contemporary Anglo-American Protestants did. "A dispensation is defined as one of the several systems or bodies of law in which at different periods God has revealed his mind and will to man, such as the Patriarchal Dispensation, the Mosaic Dispensation, or the Christian Dispensation," Roberts said. Many Protestants held that during each dispensation, God related to human beings in a somewhat different way, and though Roberts explained that in each dispensation there were common features—"the giving out or dispensing to them the word of God; the revealing to men in whole or in part the principles and ordinances of the Gospel; the conferring of divine authority upon certain chosen ones"—he allowed for distinctions in how each dispensation functioned.[19]

In contrast, the guiding principle of Joseph Fielding Smith's theory of history was not dispensational in the sense that Roberts meant. Roberts's story of dispensations was progressive. Fielding Smith's was frozen in a series of cycles. He believed that gospel "principles are eternal." By "eternal," he meant not simply omnipresent, but also unchanging. "The gospel was taught in the beginning and was declared from generation to generation," he insisted. "The plan of salvation was taught to Adam."[20] He stated flatly in *Man: His Origin and Destiny* that "Divine revelation admits of no change."[21]

Numerous times throughout his life he made clear how precise and exact he believed that adjective *eternal* to be. For instance, he believed that the organization of the LDS Church as he experienced it was identically reproduced across all of human history. Whenever there was legitimate

Christianity, there was the same Church. In a speech delivered at Brigham Young University, he claimed that, while some Christians believed that the record in the Gospel of Matthew of Christ telling Peter that "upon this rock I will build my church" gave power to Peter alone, it was not so. Rather, he claimed that the New Testament apostleship functioned identically to that in the contemporary LDS Church. "This commission was given to the entire Twelve," he explained. "Each received the fullness of the apostleship so that each, should the time come, could serve as the senior, or president of the Church in his turn." He also explained that Peter, James, and John were "the forerunner of the First Presidency in our day."[22]

Such beliefs extended beyond the line of priestly authority and organization to practices and culture. When one correspondent asked Fielding Smith whether the various ritual sacraments as the Saints practiced them were done in the ancient world, Fielding Smith replied that they were. "Baptism was practiced among the Jews," he explained. "Baptism was taught to Adam, and he was commanded to teach it to his children." And, more than this, he asserted that all the ritual practices of his Church were known as far back as Adam. "The detailed history of the performance of the saving ordinances of the gospel as practiced in ancient times was never recorded in any detail, because such ordinances are sacred and not for the world," he said. But more, "Scribes and translators took from the record the plain and precious parts because they were contrary to their beliefs or comprehension."[23]

To a correspondent confused about how to square the Epistle to Titus 3:9 ("But avoid foolish questions, and genealogies, and contentions, and strivings about the law; for they are unprofitable and vain," as the King James Version has it) with the Latter-day Saints' practice of family history research, Fielding Smith explained that Paul was an avid genealogist. "Perhaps we do not have the full text of Paul's instruction to Timothy and Titus," he speculated. "We may be sure, however, that he would not take a stand in opposition to the teachings of the prophets who went before him. Genealogical research must have been done in the days of Paul which he did not condemn."[24]

Origins

"It is natural for man to worship, no matter where they live, or when," Fielding Smith wrote. He believed that human beings were naturally religious because God had given Adam a perfect system of faith.[25] In that claim,

Fielding Smith placed himself within a wide and motley stream of mid-century scholars and writers who were skeptical of the modern idea that progressive evolution might explain social development.

The scholar of religion Mircea Eliade, for instance, argued that the human religious impulse was in fact a timeless universal, a coherent facet of the human experience rooted in the desire to return to a mythic origin. It was an interpretation that the LDS scholar Hugh Nibley, an associate of Fielding Smith, seized on to argue that all human religions were fragmented reflections of the ancient religion God gave to Adam. The German Catholic priest Wilhelm Schmidt argued similarly to Nibley. His work was quite important to Fielding Smith. The two were the same age, and Schmidt spent many years in ethnographic study of Indigenous peoples in Oceania and Africa. By the 1930s, Schmidt had begun publishing in English a series of books arguing that, in fact, contrary to Tylor and other "civilization" theorists, monotheism was the oldest form of religion on earth. "Primitive belief in a Supreme Being," Schmidt wrote, "is an essential property . . . of the most ancient of human cultures."[26] Fielding Smith cited him repeatedly.

Fielding Smith also leaned—as did many Latter-day Saint thinkers—on J. P. Maclean, a Universalist minister and archaeologist. In 1879, while still in his early thirties, Maclean published *The Mound Builders*, a study of the great constructed mounds white settlers discovered in the Ohio Valley. Mclean argued that, unlike contemporary Native Americans, "the Mound Builders grew out of a state of savagism. When they left the Valley of the Ohio they were no longer barbarians, but were making rapid strides toward a higher state of existence." He credited the quality of their tools, evidence of a complex form of government, and their religious life, which he believed to be advanced. His studies revealed their "object of worship, from a low form, ultimately becomes an invisible spiritual presence."[27]

Though Maclean took so many of the ideas and arguments of conventional civilization theory for granted, his work presented a simple conundrum—the Mound Builders were a more advanced civilization than Maclean's contemporary Native Americans, yet somehow they had been supplanted. "What became of them?" Maclean asked, in puzzlement. He did not take seriously the notion that the ancestors of the very Native peoples he saw around him were capable of building such mounds because of his belief that civilization was an ascending ladder. Instead, Maclean theorized the Mound Builders were driven from Ohio by assaults from "semicivilized" peoples. Maclean's book closes with speculation that the Mound Builders renewed their civilization in Central America, building the great monumental structures Europeans found there.[28] To Latter-day Saints, it was obvious—Maclean had discovered archaeological evidence of the Book of Mormon.

The story of the Mound Builders as Maclean understood it fits into the patterns of history that Schmidt believed in. They were also the patterns of history Fielding Smith found in the Book of Mormon. Rather than a steady ascent gained through education, cultivation of virtue, and reason, Schmidt and Maclean presented history as teetering between stasis and decline.[29]

Lineage

Perhaps the most dramatic illustration of divine management of human history was the cluster of concepts Fielding Smith named lineage. His lifelong devotion to genealogical work made the idea of family central to his theology. In *Salvation Universal*, a tract he had compiled from lectures he gave in his position as an official of the Genealogical Society, he taught that one of the basic principles of human salvation was that "Adam our father should come to this earth and stand at the head of the whole human family." The work of salvation, indeed, was simply the reconstituting of that primal family, which was why Fielding Smith insisted that his faith was "broader and more liberal in our teachings" than any other Christian faith, who would "reject the vast majority of this human family" for individual failures.[30] His beliefs about family, then, also shaped his beliefs about human history.

He formulated the concept of lineage most dramatically in his ideas about people of Black African descent. Since Church president Brigham Young's 1852 decree that such people could not be ordained to the priesthood, their opportunities for participation in the Church had steadily narrowed. Exclusion from priesthood office was followed by exclusion from temple worship, policies formalized by Fielding Smith's father while he served as president of the Church. During that period, various leaders of the Church offered a wide range of racist justifications for the policy. Brigham Young claimed that Black people were descended from Cain and thus could not hold the priesthood for that reason. Other early leaders in the Church speculated that Black people possessed spirits that were less righteous in human beings' premortal existence and thus were cursed to lose privileges while on earth.[31]

By the time of Fielding Smith's maturity, many Church leaders had fused the two ideas. B. H. Roberts, for instance, explained that Cain's descendants were "that race . . . through which it is ordained those spirits that were not valiant in the great rebellion in heaven should come."[32]

This racist reconciliation appealed to Fielding Smith for reasons he explained to his son, that Black people "are not being punished for something that Cain did." Rather, "they were not entitled to take white bodies. This is because they exercised their agency in the spirit world." In this way, Fielding Smith reconciled his stern imperative for moral choice with his surety that God alone controlled the arc of human history.[33]

In his 1931 treatise *The Way to Perfection*, Fielding Smith linked his ideas about Black people to a broader racist theology of lineage that sought to reconcile free will and divine governance over history. He asserted first that all human spirits were graded in premortal life. "Some were more intelligent than others, some more faithful, while some actually rebelled," he said. Fielding Smith believed that a whole host of circumstances that atheists might believe to be the product of social evolution or free will were determined before one was born. "Our place among the tribes and nations evidently was assigned to us by the Lord," he wrote. "Certain spirits were chosen to come through the lineage of Abraham," a selection Fielding Smith deemed a great reward. Similarly, he said, it was "reasonable to believe that less worthy spirits would come through less favored lineage."[34]

In this way, Fielding Smith could reconcile his belief in God's fairness with the evident injustice of the world he saw around him; for him, pain and unfairness could ultimately be ascribed to the immutable justice of God. His certainty that God's house was a house of order led him to discount historical evidence that contradicted his beliefs. His selectivity should not be taken as simple sloppiness but rather a reflection of his intellectual priorities, his comfort with racist hierarchies that reflected his faith in an ordered universe, and his certainty that information he believed to be revelatory trumped more human ways of knowing, like the methods of the discipline of history.

In October 1959, Fielding Smith wrote to Mrs. Doyle Nunley, who had asked him about the "story of the ordained Negro." The reference was to Elijah Abel, a Black man ordained to priestly office in 1836 with Joseph

Smith's approval.[35] Fielding Smith, however, followed his father's conclusions. Based on faulty testimony from another Church member, Joseph F. Smith decided that his own uncle Joseph Smith taught that Black men should never be ordained to the priesthood. Fielding Smith repeated that story to Nunley, writing that while some Church members had wanted to ordain Abel, "they took this matter to the Prophet Joseph Smith [who] said it was wrong and that Negroes could not hold the priesthood." Fielding Smith went on to explain that though the historical record showed that Abel had been set apart as a Seventy and served a mission, "there were two or three men named Elijah Abel, one of them filled a mission and was set apart by my father, but he was not a Negro."[36] Fielding Smith's history here was incorrect—perhaps influenced by conflicting spellings of Abel's name in the historical record—but it reflected his convictions that history must fit the stable order he believed God had ordained for it.

At the same time, lineage was not merely an explanation for disadvantage. As Fielding Smith explained lineage to his son, he reminded him to be grateful to have "a white body and are preaching the Gospel, because you merited this blessing before you were born, having been faithful in the spirit existence."[37] Fielding Smith took seriously the Bible's obsession with genealogy, patriarchy, and primogeniture. Its stories of inheritance and fathers and sons described for him a universe of order and hierarchy that he prized, and he easily transmuted such ideas onto the status quo of white supremacy in the Church.

"The patriarchal order, or that which is called the right of primogeniture, is fast fading away," Fielding Smith commented. "In its stead republican forms of government are being established." Government by a righteous patriarch was the ideal order, that which God intended, but republican forms of government were a necessary fallback because human sin ensured it was impossible to guarantee that fathers and sons could be righteous. The Church for Fielding Smith was one of the few human institutions where that order might be preserved. He pointed to several offices in the Church that still passed from father to son; that of patriarch to the Church and the presidency of the Aaronic priesthood. Though the latter was merely theoretical and the former would change soon after Fielding Smith died, he believed it was essential to keep this ancient, and to his mind divine, model alive. After all, he believed that in heaven God governed through righteous patriarchy.[38]

52

For Fielding Smith, then, the story of human history was not the story of development and progress; rather, it was the story of various races enacting those fates God already expected. At the beginning of his book *The Progress of Man*, Fielding Smith scoffed at the conventional story that "after many millenniums of progress . . . gradually man progressed, increasing in knowledge and power, until he reached the wonderful state of intelligence which he possessed today. This is a very pretty story with just one defect—it is not true!" Instead, he insisted, "human nature has not changed in the past six thousand years of the earth's temporal existence" and, therefore, "culture and ignorance have run in parallel directions at the same time."[39] The belief that seemed second nature to so many theorists that a democratic civilization would also be advanced in terms of morality or government was a confusion that masked the truth that all civilizations always stood on the brink of moral failure.

All these arguments find expression in Fielding Smith's discussion of the European conquest of the Americas. He rejected the notion that the event was a triumph of progress and civilization over ignorance. Rather, it was a morally dubious consequence of technical supremacy. Indeed, in this particular case, Fielding Smith believed the Europeans had it backward. "Europeans looked upon the Lamanites who possessed the American continent as being savages and as such not entitled to any rights of possession," he observed. Instead, these Europeans were ignorant of the fact that God had guided the Indigenous peoples of the Americas to that continent. Therefore, he wrote, "The Indians would have had as good a right had they sailed to the shores of Europe and planted their standard by right of force or supposed superior civilization. Force is not justice." For Fielding Smith, contemporary Western nations might be advanced technically, but they were nonetheless afflicted with "greed and selfish jealousy . . . the love of pleasure and the seeking of power that does not come from enlightenment or superior civilization." In fact, Fielding Smith wrote, the Book of Mormon taught that "there were in America civilizations even at the time of discovery just as far advanced in many particulars as the so-called Christian nations of Europe."[40]

Fielding Smith's belief in lineage and family derived in part from his haunted relationship with his own ancestors. His sense of destined responsibility coupled with defiant pride led Fielding Smith to frequently discuss his own lineage and to emphasize the significance of the Smith family not simply to the Church of Jesus Christ of Latter-day Saints but to God's plan for humanity in total. When he was ninety-four years old and near the end of his life, he spoke to a congregation gathered to hear him in Oahu. "The prophet Joseph Smith is my great Uncle. His brother, Hyrum Smith, the Patriarch, is my grandfather. These two good men sealed their testimony with their blood," he told an audience who undoubtedly already knew. "In the course of time I expect to see both the Prophet Joseph Smith and my grandfather Hyrum Smith. I am grateful that I shall be able to report to them that the great work for which they laid down their lives is continuing to roll forward."[41]

Fielding Smith believed, and often stated, that the Smith family was literally descended from Ephraim, the son of Joseph of Egypt, and founder of one of the twelve tribes of Israel. "The Lord designated or made it known by revelation that the Prophet Joseph Smith was of that family, the descendant of Ephraim," he told a lecture hall at BYU in 1956. This of course meant that the prophet's father was as well, which is why Joseph Smith Sr. became the first patriarch of the church. "For that reason the Patriarchal Priesthood was conferred upon him with the commandment that it should be handed down from father to son," Fielding Smith said of the prophet's father.[42]

Fielding Smith also believed that lineage governed the membership of the Church itself. He wrote to his son, "The people we are gathering today into the Church are most entirely Israelites who have mixed with the Gentile nations. . . . Most of them are Ephraimites by descent."[43] Ephraim, he said, had a special mission, "to minister to his fellows of the other tribes, including gathered Judah." For Fielding Smith, all Latter-day Saints heard and responded to the message of the Church because it resonated, quite literally, with their blood.[44] Their lineage had prepared and equipped them, just as he believed the spiritual lineage of Black people handicapped them.

Similar questions of divine lineage and premortal choices shaped his interaction with other "races" he encountered. He sympathized with his son Milton, sent to Argentina on a mission, assuring him that "there is some blood of Israel in that country," despite the seeming dominance of Roman Catholicism. Similarly, while his son Douglas served a mission on his own, Fielding Smith visited with a Native American congregation of the Church in South Carolina. "Since you are asking about some beautiful girl, we might send you down there when you come home. This is no joke," Fielding Smith wrote to his son. "They are very fine and refined people," he said, explaining that many members of that congregation had married white people. "Their children are part of them Lamanites and part of them white," he said, invoking an old Latter-day Saint tradition that identified Native Americans with Book of Mormon peoples descended from Israelites and that promised that their skin would be lightened as they became faithful.[45]

This sort of racism, conflating racial identity with religious identity, was common in the late nineteenth century, sometimes in tension with but more often in concert with the sort of evolutionary theory that dominated the age. Fielding Smith's particularly Latter-day Saint manifestation of it owed a great deal to a larger theory popularly called "British Israelism," or "Anglo-Israelism," the belief that white northern Europeans were actually the descendants of the twelve tribes of Israel. By the 1930s, British Israelite conventions were attracting thousands of members of the Church of England and other Protestant groups to gatherings in London. British Israelism also blended two imperatives that many British and American people were feeling at the time: the desire to justify their colonial domination of many nations in the global south, but also to spread Christianity. John Gilder Shaw, a passionate British Israelism theorist, pled with "the British race to open their eyes to the glorious truth that we are in the possession of all the blessings promised to Abraham and his posterity."[46] For white Latter-day Saints like Joseph Fielding Smith, belief that his was an Ephraimite Church contributed to his racism.

Ethical Monotheism, the Bible, and the Book of Mormon

The German scholar Julius Wellhausen became famous in the late nineteenth century as one of the deans of the new higher criticism, a school of academics who sought to evaluate the Bible in its historical context. Wellhausen's work remains the classic formulation of the documentary hypothesis, the theory that the first five books of the Hebrew Bible, from Genesis through Deuteronomy, are the work of an editor or group of editors who redacted together many early sources. But Wellhausen also posited that this redaction reflected the theories of civilization he and so many others in his time were immersed in.

For Wellhausen, the history of the Israelite people as described in the Hebrew Bible was the story of progress from primitive animism to what he called ethical monotheism. The religion of the Israelites evolved from ritual worship of a local nature deity to the great prophets like Jeremiah and Isaiah, who taught of a single transcendent deity over all humanity who valued moral behavior more than ceremonies. This ethical monotheism was redeemed in the teachings of Jesus in the New Testament. For Protestants like Wellhausen, true Christianity (by which they meant Protestant Christianity, which deemphasized ritual and emphasized good behavior) was therefore genuine religion.[47]

Wellhausen's narrative appealed a great deal to American Protestants, who found the notion of evolution a compelling way to explain their own presumed superiority over other cultures and religious groups. As Harry Emerson Fosdick, one of the leading American liberal Protestants of the early twentieth century, said of biblical scholarship like Wellhausen's, "We are saved by it from the old and impossible attempt to harmonize the Bible with itself." It "restores to us the whole book seen as a unified development from early and simple beginnings to a great conclusion."[48] Fosdick and other liberal Protestants imagined themselves the heirs of Jeremiah and Isaiah, their religion a simple, rational impulse to ethical behavior and the logical endpoint of the religious evolution the whole text taught. For them, Wellhausen had saved the Bible from irrelevance.

Joseph Fielding Smith was most distressed as such ideas began appearing in the theology of other Latter-day Saints. In the years from 1907 to 1909, BYU president George Brimhall hired two sets of brothers—Joseph and Henry Peterson and Ralph and William Chamberlin—to teach a variety of courses in psychology, biology, and philosophy. Within a year, a furor erupted. These professors, particularly the Chamberlins, taught not simply the higher criticism, but a Wellhausenian conception of religious evolution. "It is only when we perceive the constant growth, the constant evolution, in the Bible and recognize in it the progressive unfolding of the Divine Will in the Hebrew race that it has the highest meaning for and can teach and stimulate us," said Ralph Chamberlin.[49] Three of the four professors were forced from employment at BYU in 1911. Joseph Fielding Smith's father, Church president Joseph F. Smith, issued a statement explaining why. The professors were teaching that "revelation combines a human element with the divine impression and should be subject to such modification" as seemed necessary as history progressed. But, the elder Smith said, "divine revelation is truth, and must abide forever."[50]

Here Fielding Smith's father enunciated a religious principle his son clung to for the rest of his life: truth was eternal and therefore evolution was incompatible with truth.

And yet, despite his father's injunction, Fielding Smith saw similar ideas emerging closer to home in the work of two other leaders of the church, Apostle John A. Widtsoe and Fielding Smith's old nemesis Seventy B. H. Roberts.

In 1908, Widtsoe published a book derived from a popular set of articles he had published in the church's magazine *Improvement Era.* Called *Joseph Smith as Scientist,* the book argued that Joseph Smith's revelations had anticipated and described many doctrines that scientists had described only after Smith's death. Central among them was what Widtsoe called "the law of evolution." Citing Herbert Spencer (whom Widtsoe called "the sanest of modern philosophers"), Widtsoe argued that it was the "greatest known fundamental law of the universe" that all things—from individual humans to entire planets—inexorably advanced in complexity. The apostle ducked the suggestion that this meant Darwin was right about the origin of species, but he did argue that Spencer's idea accurately described human progression from a preexistence through earth life through exaltation in a life to come.[51]

Widtsoe also argued that Spencer's rules held true in human history, which he said was a story of "progressive development." He shared Fielding Smith's basic premise that the Gospel was taught in full to Adam, Moses, and others and then lost. But he also believed—as did many American Protestants—that history was trending upward, that human beings were improving. Each restoration of truth was more developed, further progressed than the one prior.[52]

Roberts agreed with Widtsoe. "The development theory of this chapter and work," he wrote in his masterwork *The Truth, the Way, the Life,* "recognizes and starts with the eternity of life—the life force and some life forms, and the possibilities of these forms, perhaps in embryonic status, or in their simplest forms (save as to man) are transplanted to newly created worlds, there to be developed each to its highest possibilities." Roberts suggested that various ancient hominids in the fossil record—from Australopithecus to the Cro-Magnons—were "pre-Adamite races" of humanity. Therefore, with "the advent of Adam, the time had come for the achievement of some special purpose in relation to man—some spiritual purpose—that brought about the Adamic dispensation." In short, in the coming of Adam and Eve, humanity had evolved to the point at which it could endure a special relationship with God.[53]

Both thinkers believed that a Spencerian form of evolution as development was an accurate way of describing human existence. Both also explicitly embraced an evolutionary theory of society that mirrored, in some ways, that of Wellhausen. For Roberts, this was particularly evident in the Book of Mormon.

Roberts was concerned with archaeological and historical studies of ancient America in part because he thought such academic work might demonstrate the historicity of the Book of Mormon. But he also believed that this evidence would allow a reading of the Book of Mormon that mirrored Wellhausen's reading of the Bible: that is, demonstrate that the Nephite and Lamanite civilizations in that book were civilizations in the full theoretical sense of the term. Proving that was valuable both in a historical and in a pastoral sense. It would not only justify the book, but Roberts also thought the progress of civilization illustrated moral laws important for Christians to understand.

Like many other historians, Roberts assumed that various aspects of civilization—technical knowledge, writing, complex government, ethical religion—went hand-in-hand. Because the Book of Mormon's Nephites had true religion, Roberts assumed that their enemies, the Lamanites, were "the very antithesis, then, of the Nephites—the one civilized, the other barbarian." The Nephites, Roberts believed, were white; the Lamanites dark-skinned; the Nephites farmers, the Lamanites hunters; the Nephites righteous and the Lamanites idolaters.[54] The Nephites had a stable language rooted in their "written literature."[55] Their civilization was "of a very high order. Not a civilization of the stone age new or old, but a [sic] iron age of civilization far advanced."[56] Such assumptions were a stumbling block for Roberts as he sought archaeological proof of the Book of Mormon. He worried that there was no evidence of smelted metals in America, despite the fact that the Nephites seemed "an iron and steel age civilization, with its attendant higher culture of a written language."⁵⁷ But the very conundrum also illustrated how he instinctively thought of societies as something that developed and degraded as species did. Evolution was written into the bones of his moral world.

Fielding Smith knew it. He understood the theories he attacked so vehemently, or at least he read them. In *Man: His Origin and Destiny*, published in 1954 after Roberts and Widtsoe were dead, Fielding Smith spent many chapters exploring the theory of evolution. He gave a passable summary of Wellhausen's work. And then he linked the two ideas together. It was important, he insisted, to recognize "the part that evolution has played in the twisting of the Bible accounts of things in the beginning."⁵⁸ The very idea of evolution corrupted not only how people understood themselves, but how they understood their histories.

In 1937, Fielding Smith sent a letter to Lynn Bennion and Franklin West, who ran the Church's educational system. He told them he wanted to stop instructors in Church schools from teaching what he called "the development view of the Hebrew religion." He told West and Bennion that the development view was premised on the idea that "the high religion of the prophets traveled out of the dark land of primitive low religion." It seemed obvious to him that this narrative would encourage students to be skeptical of various aspects of biblical religion that scholars deemed primitive. Fielding Smith worried for the fate of the Book of Genesis, the Exodus from Egypt, and perhaps eventually even the veracity of the four gospels in the church's classrooms if such curriculum persisted. "Where, then, am I to draw the line?" he asked the commissioners. "Only that which is reasonable, or which is confirmed by the teachings of science?" It did not seem particularly reasonable to him for scholars to call primitive ancient civilizations like the Israelites and the Nephites—civilizations that Fielding Smith believed possessed all the knowledge of the gospel of Jesus Christ.⁵⁹

Fielding Smith believed such views were doing damage to the world around him. As he wrote his most important books on human history in the 1930s and 1940s—*The Progress of Man*, a distillation of history from Adam and Eve to the present, *The Signs of the Times,* a meditation on the apocalypse, and *The Way to Perfection,* a refutation of the notion of progress—he was, like most other Americans, dismayed by the Great Depression and World War II. And he was growing increasingly certain that the return of Jesus Christ was imminent.

End Times

Fielding Smith's model for history was drawn from the Hebrew Bible and the Book of Mormon, scriptural narratives that linked the health of a society directly to its devotion to God, a devotion ultimately impossible to complete because of human frailty and weakness. Book of Mormon peoples, he wrote, "reached great heights of prosperity and civilization." They also "sank in the depths of degradation and lost divine favor."[60] During the gloomy days of World War II, he counseled his son Douglas that such cycles were irresistible. "The vast majority of the inhabitants of this earth have always been those whose deeds were evil, and they are the people of the world. Since the fall of Adam this earth has been dominated by the inhabitants of the telestial order," he explained. "Every time man has take[n] government into his own hands . . . man has made a failure of it."[61]

This sort of pessimism was not uncommon in the first half of the twentieth century, particularly in the dark days of the 1930s and 1940s. In a way, Smith was not far from the neo-orthodox movement in American Protestantism, which sought to temper liberal optimism about humanity. Its leading American theologian, Reinhold Niebuhr, warned at roughly the same time Smith was writing that "History proves that the power of government is morally ambiguous. It may on occasion imperil not evil but good works. The best possible government cannot completely escape from such a possibility."[62] One of Fielding Smith's own conclusions sounded a great deal like Niebuhr's endorsement of humility: "Each age considers itself modern, progressive, and wiser than the one that went before; but is it not possible that the present age also cherishes many foolish notions that may be ridiculed by the generations yet to come?"[63]

Despite such affinities, Fielding Smith would have found Niebuhr, who was willing to read biblical miracles in symbolic and moral terms, theologically unacceptable. But others closer to Fielding Smith were also echoing the great theologian. Sin and human frailty were widely emphasized principles among American Christians in the mid-twentieth century, and Protestants more conservative than Niebuhr were similarly skeptical of the possibility that human government could do good. In many ways, such worries were the reflection of the emerging power of the officially Soviet Union in the late 1940s. The Soviet domination of Eastern Europe and its successful testing of a nuclear weapon in 1949 inaugurated the Cold War, and many American

Christians believed that Soviet power signaled a global declension of true faith.

Carl Henry, the intellectual leader of white conservative evangelicalism in those days, mused that "human depravity often translates the centralization of power into tyrannical oppression."[64] For many theologically conservative evangelicals, mistrust of human sinfulness led naturally to political conservatism and fear of the state, particularly during President Franklin Roosevelt's New Deal—attitudes that Fielding Smith shared. He dolefully observed to his son in the military that that the Germans thought Adolf Hitler was a "savior. I regret to say that many, very many people in the US looked upon Roosevelt in much the same way." In consequence, he said, "we are in the hands of the Communists and I am fearful that the people who respect constitutional government are outnumbered."[65]

It was common for Fielding Smith to insist that the ancients, the figures he read about in the Bible, were actually more advanced than his contemporaries. In a 1942 series of radio addresses on the consummation of human history, Fielding Smith insisted, "These men were not ignorant superstitious old fogies with minds prejudiced by false notions and imaginations and traditions inherited from ancestors who came down from the monkey stage," again linking the falsity of the theory of evolution to false beliefs about social development. Rather, "the decline of knowledge both spiritual and temporal, including the false notions regarding the earth and the universe, came about through rebellion and rejection of the commandments of the Lord."[66]

The sole difference between the two ages was technology, and Fielding Smith believed that such advances were not the result of human ingenuity or improvement but rather divine intervention. Most civilizational theorists believed that technological or social progress were the products of moral development and that all such advances supported each other. Progress in science—for instance, the development of the printing press—would, they thought, naturally lead to progress in other arenas. The printing press would foster democratic government and Protestant religion. The historian John Fiske, a favorite in the early twentieth century, made such an argument in his history of Puritan New England.[67]

Fielding Smith, on the other hand, rejected such arguments as the application of evolutionism to human history. "Abraham, as he sat in his tent, could not receive the news of the world published in the daily press and have it delivered to him at his door; he could not push a button and turn on the electric light, but is that saying that Abraham was less intelligent than men are who dwell on the earth today?" Fielding Smith demanded. "The truth of the matter is that these things were not intended for Abraham's day, and they would not be known and utilized today if the Lord had not revealed them."[68]

In the aftermath of World War II, Fielding Smith was growing certain that the rapid technological progress he saw around him was a sign from God. Some found hope and optimism in incredible improvements in media, medicine, and transport; the space race captured many Americans' imaginations. But, as his response to the Apollo missions indicated, Fielding Smith thought that such seeming advances should actually warn of peril. To him, they were a sign that God was wrapping up history. "The time has come for this wonderful development in science, art, mechanics, medicine, etc., to be made known and given to the world for the benefit of man, and this not due to the superiority of intellect, but because the Lord has willed it," he told a radio audience in 1942.[69] These developments were happening because God now intended to fulfill final promises that required them before human history ended.

For instance, Fielding Smith believed that the development of microfilm and computerized databases had occurred in order to facilitate the work of genealogy and the temple ordinances that he believed must be performed for the dead. He told the story several times of meeting a lawyer who had become intensely fascinated with his family history and who could say only "Something is impelling me to do it." Fielding Smith tried to convert him, to no avail. But, nonetheless, he demanded, "Does anyone wish to tell me that this influence of the Spirit of the Lord has not influenced these people?"[70]

Similarly, he believed that modern communications technology was developed to foster the spread of the Church. He noted that the early Church settled into apostasy because its members were not "kept in communication with the General Authorities of the Church." And to compensate for the problem, "when the Lord saw fit to bring it about, he again revived the minds of men" and inspired the creation of the printing press, which prepared the way for Joseph Smith's production of the Book of Mormon. The radio had been invented in the twentieth century for "the fulfilling of this prediction that the Gospel must be preached in all the world." God had begun to create "many agencies to bring to pass his prophecies."[71]

Precisely what those prophecies were, Fielding Smith had a great hand in sorting out for Latter-day Saints. Early Mormonism was quite millenarian, which is to say interested in the Second Coming and the great social transformations that would accompany it. Like many other Americans, they worried about the spiritual decay that they believed beset American society, but they also believed that the building of the Zion community of their Church would give them a bulwark against it as they waited for Christ to come and finally set things right. But these topics gradually fell from favor in the Church in the early twentieth century as its members increasingly assimilated with American society generally.[72]

With his 1942 series of lectures and the subsequent volume *The Signs of the Times*, Fielding Smith renewed the emphasis with vigor. He brought to the topic his own theological preoccupations and interests, repeating much of what Latter-day Saints and other American Christians had been saying since the nineteenth century. But he also was immersed in the booming world discussing end-times prophecies that was sweeping the United States in the 1920s and 1930s, and his arguments took on the cast of many conservative evangelicals who, in those years, were in a particularly apocalyptic fervor. For Fielding Smith, precise explication of what the Second Coming would bring was in line with his vision of history as the acts of God, not efforts by human beings.

"Today a great many people are talking about Daniel and what Daniel has said, and the whole 11th chapter of Daniel and some things in the 12th," Fielding Smith observed in a lecture delivered in November 1942.[73] The eleventh chapter of Daniel describes a series of kings—a king of the South, a king of the North, a series of successors and alliances, blasphemies, and power—and a great battle joined when the king of the North invades Israel. The twelfth chapter promises a "time of trouble" and makes an ambiguous promise of how long all this chaos will last. In the King James Version that Fielding Smith would have used, the chapter speaks of "a time, times, and half a time"; it states that the "abomination of desolation" will last for "one thousand, two hundred, and ninety days."

The "great many people" Fielding Smith was alluding to in 1942 were a group of white evangelical Protestants, growing in numbers in the South but centered on a handful of congregations and educational institutions in urban America, like the Moody Bible Institute in Chicago or the Bible Institute of Los Angeles. Many would have called themselves fundamentalists, a term that increasingly implied devotion to premillennial dispensationalism.[74]

Premillennial dispensationalism refers to a combination of beliefs about history and the Second Coming. Dispensationalists believe in shifting periods of God's relationship with humanity across history. Premillennialists believe that Jesus Christ's coming will inaugurate the thousand-year period of peace predicted in the Book of Revelation that will precede the Last Judgment of humanity. These beliefs and many like them have been held in many configurations throughout Christian history, but, beginning in the late nineteenth century, a particular style of premillennial dispensationalism began to spread in Great Britain and the United States. It was based on the teachings of the Irish evangelist John Nelson Darby, a Protestant minister who began piecing together a complex road map of the various dispensations of human history and a sketch of what he believed would happen at the end of those dispensations—a period he called the Tribulation, a terrifying but relatively brief time of anarchy and chaos on earth that would end when Christ returns to earth in triumph to begin the millennium. Darby's formulations made premillennialist dispensationalists increasingly pessimistic about the course of human history.[75]

By the 1930s, Darby's form of eschatology—the term for theorizing about the end times—had left a deep mark on American Christianity. By the 1870s, prophecy conferences held across the United States were already attracting thousands of attendees. During World War I, interest in prophecy spiked; a half-dozen major prophecy magazines saw their circulation surge. Two particular events that occurred as the war was winding down energized premillennialists: first, in 1917, communist revolutionaries seized power in the Russian Empire and, second, the next year British troops took Jerusalem from the Ottoman Empire, a military victory accompanied with an announcement from British foreign secretary Arthur Balfour that Britain intended to establish a homeland for the Jewish people. These things captured the imagination of Darby's followers because they had long been warning of a treacherous, unholy, "king of the North," as described in Daniel, and hoping for the restoration of Jewish people to Jerusalem, which they believed to be prophesied in the New Testament. In November 1918, a major prophecy conference attracted thousands of people to New York City's Carnegie Hall, US President Woodrow Wilson sent greetings to be read from the stand, and speakers assured the crowd that current events were clearly described in the Bible.[76]

By the 1920s and 1930s, evangelical premillennialists were perfecting a careful mapping out of the future from the text of the Bible and Darby's writings. Fielding Smith's form of eschatology echoed it in at least three ways. According to this narrative, in a world increasingly wracked by natural disasters, famine, plague, and instability, two dark figures would emerge—a false prophet and an evil political leader—who would promise peace. One of these figures would be the antichrist, a demonic figure set on destroying faith in God. He would create a great union of nations, and eventually turn his attention to the Jews newly returned to Israel. Dispensationalists expected that some Jews would by then be listening to Christian preachers and beginning to worship Jesus Christ. Alarmed, the antichrist would command the Jews to worship him instead; when they inevitably refused, dispensationalists expected him to mass armies around Israel, but particularly in the north. When the forces of good and evil met in the valley of Armageddon in northern Israel, Christ would descend personally from the clouds, smash the power of the antichrist, and inaugurate a peaceful millennium under his personal reign.[77]

This story is nowhere laid out in its whole anywhere in the Bible. Rather, it is stitched together from references throughout the Hebrew Bible and the New Testament. That is to say, the dispensationalist scheme depends on proof-texting—quite literally, lining up quotations from passages of scripture hundreds of pages apart. A passage from William Blackstone's 1908 book *Jesus Is Coming*, one of the most influential premillennialist books of its time, offers a good example. Arguing that Christ will reign personally on the earth after the battle of Armageddon, Blackstone writes, "'A king shall reign in righteousness.' (Isa. 32:1; Jer. 23:1–6), 'upon the throne of David' 'in Jerusalem.' (Isa. 9:7; Jer. 3:17) The apostles shall sit upon the twelve thrones (Mat. 19:28), and the Saints shall reign upon the earth Rev. 5:10."[78]

This thorough, exhaustive assemblage of a host of quotations from throughout scripture presumed that the Bible was not a collection of documents written years apart with sometimes different intents, but a single text with one unified and clear meaning, discernible to those who read it correctly. Of course, this was precisely how Joseph Fielding Smith read scripture. His writings on the Second Coming bear the mark of Darbyite dispensationalism, not simply because of its argument but also because of its method. In his lectures, he tells his audience that "I am going to go through these scriptures, from Isaiah through to Zechariah, and take them in order"; after that, he leaps from Isaiah chapter 34 to Jeremiah 25, from

Ezekiel 38 and 39 to Daniel 11 and 12, in much the same way that dispensationalists did.[79]

Of course, LDS leaders had long partaken in widely shared interpretations of particular Bible passages most American Christians interpreted as references to the Second Coming. Fielding Smith cited Parley P. Pratt's interpretation of Ezekiel, for instance, and Joseph Smith had famously invoked Daniel and described the Angel Moroni reeling off a host of proof-texted apocalyptic passages from the Bible in one of his earliest visions. Fielding Smith drew on these examples.[80]

And yet the story Fielding Smith told about the end times in the 1930s and 1940s strongly resembled that of evangelical dispensationalists in key events and content. Like them, he was taken with Britain's promise to restore a Jewish homeland and believed it would inaugurate an imminent and great war—so much so that he expanded his lectures after the creation of the State of Israel for a new edition of the book. He excitedly wrote to his son Douglas that the land in Palestine "belongs to Israel, not only the Jews," predicting that soon Latter-day Saint missionaries would be restoring the true covenant of Abraham there. Like dispensationalists, he speculated about the identity of a great opponent to God, musing that many people thought it was likely Hitler. The story Fielding Smith told about the end times during World War II, then, bore a great resemblance to the dispensationalist story of the Tribulation being told at the same time. For both, the nations of the world would be assembled in a great war against Israel, and the Jews would be saved by the sudden coming of Christ.[81]

But, in the end, perhaps the greatest resemblance, and the hardest to quantify, between Fielding Smith's work on the end times and that of dispensationalists is its mood. Early Mormon apocalypticism promised a twin outpouring of wrath on a sinful world but also a promise of a coming utopia. Early Mormons believed that chaos was coming but also that God had promised to his faithful people that they would be protected and preserved through the cataclysms.[82]

By the 1930s and 1940s, though, that sense of physical and spiritual separation from the rest of the world had faded and with it any sense of special security. Certainly, Fielding Smith's own life showed its absence. His son Lewis was killed in combat in January 1945. Fielding Smith had feared this. In the fall of 1944 he wrote to his son Douglas, also a soldier, that he was "certainly grateful when Lewis was transferred from a bomber" to a hopefully safer job. After he received word of Lewis's death, he wrote bitterly to Douglas that "we do not belong to the world, but we are in it, and are subject to its dictation." He told his son—for what must have been the thousandth time—about the assassinations of Hyrum and Joseph Smith. He compared the "howling mob" that killed them to "the treatment now being given some of our people by the Japanese and I fear by the Germans."[83]

The worst part was, he told his sons, Americans deserved it. To Lewis he wrote, "We are fighting for the liberty and rights of peoples, yet we cannot boast of our faithfulness or willingness to keep the commandments the Lord has given us." To Douglas he said, "This is a wicked world. It does not grow better but each day is approaching the goal of destruction." Postmillennialists—those who believed that Christ would come once the gospel had filled the whole earth—were simply kidding themselves. "Many people think he is going to come when the people are ready to receive him," he told Douglas. "If he had to wait until that time then he would never come."[84] Even Latter-day Saints were no better. "It is a shame that all of our boys will not keep themselves straight and true but unfortunately there are some who will not," he wrote. "Some also have been a disgrace to their Church." If New York City was "of the wicked cities of the world . . . our own little burg is getting to be a place we need not brag about."[85]

With the death of Lewis, but more, the simple spread of vice among his own people, the world had found its way to Joseph Fielding Smith, and the pessimism that resulted bolstered his sympathies for premillennialism, his conviction that human progress was a myth, and that human beings would do best to trust that God held firm the wheel of history. To believe otherwise, to his mind, was to tempt inevitable disaster.

CHAPTER FOUR

Orthodoxy

At one point during his mission in Nottingham, England, Joseph Fielding Smith drafted a letter that he sent to roughly two hundred Protestant ministers serving in the greater Nottingham area. He included a tract from the Church of Jesus Christ of Latter-day Saints. The letter invited the ministers to "peruse these principles carefully, and compare them with the Holy Bible to see if they do not agree with that sacred record." Fielding Smith invited the ministers to send him materials about the "fundamental principles of your own faith, which, I promise you, I will carefully read." He hoped to spark an exchange that would clearly delineate the doctrinal distinctions between his own faith and the Protestant Christianity of central England.[1]

Few actually replied, which Fielding Smith expected. "I think they have had their heads together to see what they could do in order to put down this strange doctrine," he wrote to his wife, Louisa. But that assumption did not seem to be borne out by the two men who responded to Fielding Smith's letter most fully. One minister, Perry Holbrook, informed Fielding Smith that "The differences which separate us are so slight and the division among Christians cause such untold harm that I earnestly wish that good and true people would be content to hold their little notions in private." He expressed pleasure that many people can "become members of the Church of England if they would be content to differ from others without separating from them." Another, Arthur Beery, told Smith of his disappointment that people "so pandered to their own wishes that we find today several hundred different sects in England all divided by circumstances rather than essentials."[2]

Even at this early point in his life, Fielding Smith seemed baffled by Christians who did not take it for granted, as he did, that being right about doctrine was central to Christian identity. But both of his correspondents were members of the Church of England, or Anglican Church, and for two centuries by that point the Church of England had been grappling with the problem of doctrinal orthodoxy. In the sixteenth and seventeenth century Anglicanism had faced an insurgent Puritan movement denouncing it for doctrinal laxity and in response the church had emphasized the importance of ritual and sacrament over orthodox belief. In the eighteenth century, the "latitudinarian movement" emerged, preaching that, as Holbrook and Beery explained to Fielding Smith, the real unity of the church was in sacramental belonging rather than theological uniformity. By the nineteenth century, as Anglicanism spread all over the globe, its leaders found wisdom in downplaying doctrinal consistency in favor of what some by then were calling the "broad church."[3]

Of course, Fielding Smith knew little of this history. But the episode marked the beginning of his sense that correct doctrine lay at the foundation of genuine Christian identity, and the next thirty years of his life only made that conviction firmer. By the 1910s, Joseph Fielding Smith had become the most prominent voice within the LDS tradition echoing Reformed Protestant arguments about the primacy of doctrine. He, like those conservative Protestants, argued that there was an essential connection between correct belief and correct behavior, that accurate theology was foundational to all else that a believer might hope to accomplish, from personal salvation to the building of a righteous society. As he grew older and rose in the ranks and in the respect of the Church of Jesus Christ of Latter-day Saints, he not only accepted but embraced the role of the guardian of Latter-day Saint orthodoxy; indeed, in a way, his insistence that the Church needed such a figure created a Church-wide belief that it did require one.

Fundamentalism, Doctrine, and Culture

In 1874, David Swing, minister of the Fourth Presbyterian Church in Chicago, was tried for heresy before the Presbytery of Chicago. He was charged with having taught that the Bible was a historical document; leaning on German biblical scholarship of the sort that had produced Julius Wellhausen, Swing told his congregation that the Bible illustrated a slow development toward the ethical religion of Jesus from a crude and primitive cult. He—and many others—were shocked when he was brought up on heresy charges. Swing said he had thought that heresy was a problem of the past and asked why, if he taught people to do good, doctrinal orthodoxy was necessary. And yet, as biblical scholarship and the new theological ideas it fostered spread across the United States, a group of Christians emerged who believed that those new ideas were a danger to true religion and who sought to police orthodoxy's boundaries. Charles A. Briggs, a Presbyterian professor at Union Theological Seminary, was convicted of heresy in 1892 for, in part, claiming that there were factual errors in the Bible and that it was a mistake to read prophecies in the Hebrew Bible as references to Jesus Christ. And on and on. Each hearing made front-page news.[4]

Such high-profile arguments mostly emerged in Protestant denominations like Presbyterianism and Congregationalism. These denominations shared two things: first, all were descended from the Calvinist branch of the Protestant Reformation. John Calvin was the most theologically passionate of the Protestant Reformers, and it was no mistake that his followers cared more than many other Christians about correct doctrine, enough to select it as a measuring rod for genuine Christianity. Second, those denominations also had the governing apparatus to hold heresy trials and establish theological expectations for ministers and members.[5]

Other denominations might lack one or the other of those things. The Baptists, for example, also were Calvinist, and many were enthusiastic theologians. (It was Baptists who made premillennial dispensationalism a phenomenon in the United States.) But Baptists had little denominational structure to enforce beliefs; each Baptist congregation decided on its own whether to affiliate with larger conventions, and even powerful conventions like the Southern Baptist Convention could do little to enforce doctrinal orthodoxy. Similarly, many non-Calvinist Christian groups in the United States were hardly invested in the importance of doctrine. Some, like the burgeoning Pentecostal movement, prized the presence of charismatic gifts of the spirit like speaking in tongues or prophecy far more than orthodox doctrine, to the point that some Pentecostals rejected the traditional Trinity. Others, like Roman Catholics or the Episcopal Church, taught that the church was bound together through rituals and sacraments, and, thus, though battles over correct doctrine sometimes appeared within their flocks, they were far more muted than they were in Calvinist denominations.[6]

It was not, then, a given that adherence to correct theology would become a flashpoint and a measure of loyalty within the Church of Jesus Christ of Latter-day Saints. But factors were pushing the Church in that direction, and Fielding Smith himself experienced some of them.

Sociologist Armand Mauss has charted the history of the LDS Church as a vacillation between assertion of distinctiveness and independence and a quest for integration and assimilation. For thinkers a generation older than Fielding Smith, like John Widtsoe and B. H. Roberts, LDS theology was a tool for expressing similarity to the larger American culture. The project of Widtsoe's *Joseph Smith as Scientist* was, as Widtsoe put it, to show that "the teachings of Joseph Smith, the Mormon Prophet, were in full harmony with the most advanced scientific thought of today, and that he anticipated the world of science in the statement of fundamental facts and theories of physics, chemistry, astronomy and biology."[7]

And yet, for Joseph Fielding Smith, the project of harmonizing Mormonism with American culture was wrongheaded from the start. He was scion of a family that had not trusted the goodwill of American culture outside the Church for a hundred years, and ever since his battles with the Reorganized Church of Jesus Christ of Latter-day Saints in the first two decades of the century, he had understood that the distinctiveness of the two movements emerged from doctrinal difference. As he wrote to the RLDS leader Richard Evans, opponents of the Latter-day Saints "fully realize their inability to successfully oppose the doctrines of the Church with truth as a weapon of attack, and, therefore, resort to falsehood." But "The doctrine of the Church has survived all such onslaughts. . . . It will continue to spread, bless mankind and prepare all who accept it, and follow its teachings in righteousness, for an inheritance in the kingdom of God."[8]

Here, Fielding Smith roots religious distinctiveness in theology and ascribes to that theology the power to effect social change, an impulse that was common in the early twentieth century. By the 1920s, the press began to fill with stories about a battle between science and religion, and a new movement of Protestants who called themselves fundamentalists began to insist that historic Christianity depended on the teaching of accurate doctrine.

The Protestants who first used the term *fundamentalist* were Baptists who meant by it something very specific. Fundamentalists were those who upheld the relatively new (but seemingly traditional) doctrine of

CH

biblical inerrancy, as well as fidelity to the reality of miracles. But scholars have observed that fundamentalists were more than simply theologians. More broadly, they were antimodernists distressed at the cultural changes sweeping across the United States in the early twentieth century. They were militant opponents of changing gender norms, of the spread of commercialized entertainment, and of the growing authority of nonreligious authorities in areas of American life like education, government, and the media. At the same time, fundamentalists were a product of modernity as well; their use of media and their application of scientific authority to scripture revealed that.[9]

Calling Joseph Fielding Smith a fundamentalist is useful in some ways but not others. On the one hand, Fielding Smith rejected absolutely many of the theological presuppositions that Protestant fundamentalists valued, and vice versa. His mode of scriptural interpretation used language similar to that of fundamentalist arguments about inerrancy and plainness but extended it. And yet he rejected any perception that his own mode of interpretation shared anything with theirs. "There are two views taken concerning the interpretation of the scriptures," he wrote. "One proclaimed by the great mother church is that there is a sure way of interpretation and this is the power vested in the pope who is infallible in such interpretation. The other view is that man must depend upon his own reason for his scriptural understanding." The first he ascribed to Roman Catholics; the second to Protestants. Unfortunately, Smith argued, both these interpretations were faulty, for "It is only natural when the heavens are closed and men are left to grope and find their way without divine aid there will be confusion." Rather, he said, scripture had to be interpreted through the lens of modern revelation. He dismissed Protestant theology generally as "one of the most pernicious doctrines ever advocated by man" and in no way perceived Protestant fundamentalists as friends to the Latter-day Saints. He warned his son serving in the military to avoid other Christians, for their "churches professing to be Christian and to be His followers . . . have taught everything else except His divine truth."[10]

And yet, Fielding Smith did share some of the characteristics of Protestant fundamentalism. He perceived most Protestant churches as his enemies and yet embraced their antimodernism. Like them, he feared and condemned most cultural changes sweeping the United States in the twentieth century, and though he considered them religious enemies, he could adopt what historian Margaret Lambert Bendroth has described as a strategy of "co-belligerence" between enemies toward a greater enemy. He made a friendly ally of George McCready Price, a Seventh-day Adventist who was one of the most ardent American opponents of geological science that suggested the earth was millions of years old, and he cited approvingly conservative Protestants and Roman Catholics who suggested, as did Fielding Smith himself, that the Western world was in decline.[11]

Perhaps most significant, Fielding Smith shared with Protestant fundamentalists the conviction that decline in social morality and cultural vitality was the child of incorrect theological belief. If we are to use the word *fundamentalist* to describe him, then, it should not simply be due to his conservative theological positions; rather, it should describe the relationship he saw between theology and the rise of a modern society he believed to be corrupt.

The Snell Case

Fielding Smith's attempt to implement doctrinal rigor and his belief in its social ramifications are most famously illustrated in the case of Heber Snell. Snell was a lanky student of the Hebrew Bible and a teacher in the Church's educational system, and something about him seemed to get under Fielding Smith's skin. Perhaps it was their aspect; both men were humorless about their religion, deadly earnest, and took it for granted that their particular readings of Mormon theology were not simply accurate, but necessary for the Church's survival.

While an undergraduate at Brigham Young University (BYU), Snell studied under Ralph and William Chamberlin, advocates of an evolutionary view of the history of religion, who eventually came under fire at the university for their theology. Snell himself began teaching in the Church's institute program in the 1930s. He also joined what has come to be known as the Chicago experiment. In the late 1920s and 1930s, the men directing the Church's educational system began dispatching their teachers to the University of Chicago divinity school, one of the preeminent programs in the country, but also one dominated by professors in the school of Wellhausen, modernist scholars who advocated the higher criticism and the developmental interpretation of biblical religion. In January 1937, Snell, then just beginning at Chicago, delivered a talk to a group of institute teachers

in which he presented such an interpretation of the Hebrew Bible, arguing for, among other points, the presence of multiple authorial voices in
the book of Isaiah, each of which expressed, to Snell's way of thinking, a
progressively more enlightened view of God.[12]

Ten years later, having received his PhD, Snell turned in a manuscript
called *Ancient Israel: Its Story and Meaning* to Franklin West, the Church
commissioner of education. West, a physicist by training, was fascinated
with Snell's theories, but he also knew the politics of the Church. He told
Snell he could not publish the volume because Joseph Fielding Smith sat
as the chairman of the Church Publications Committee and on the Church
Board of Education. West knew that Fielding Smith, if he read the book,
would never allow it to be published. So Snell ended up publishing the
book on his own with a small Salt Lake City press. It received a respect-
ful response from academic scholars of the Bible, but Snell was proud of
his work and wanted more. He began pushing for endorsements from
West, from George Albert Smith, then president of the Church, and other
church leaders, hoping that the book might be used at BYU and elsewhere
in the Church despite what Fielding Smith might want. It was not simple
self-aggrandizement on Snell's part; rather, he seemed certain that, as he
told Earl Harmer, who wrote to Snell lambasting the book, that its critics
"missed its great themes and the heavy support it gives to fundamental LDS
theology. From beginning to end the book speaks of a personal God."[13]

Snell seemed somewhat baffled that people like Harmer and Fielding
Smith found his book distressing. He was earnestly, thoroughly convinced
that if he simply pleaded his case vividly enough, his critics would become
friends. It did not happen, and at times he admitted it. "I have never been
as wise in my public utterances as I should have been," he wrote to the
Church Board of Education in response to criticism of his teaching that
the board received from students. But he defended his writing and teaching as necessary to save the younger generations of the Church. "Many of
our young people are not zealous for God and the Church. Should we not
utilize science and history to help them?" he wrote to the board. "We had
better do it for their sakes, even though doing so requires us to yield up
some unimportant traditional interpretations."[14]

Ancient Israel: Its Story and Meaning was a fairly conventional synthesis
of the work of many Protestant scholars of the Bible. It leaned extensively
on the work of scholars like Yale professor Charles F. Kent—a leading

74

74

proponent of the notion that the Bible told a story of a civilization that rose from savagery to a proto-Protestantism—and Chicago professor J. M. P. Smith, himself a graduate of Chicago's divinity school, whose book *The Moral Life of the Hebrews* celebrated "the great progress made by the Hebrews in their thousand years of moral discipline." These men argued, following the German biblical scholar Julius Wellhausen, that ancient Israelite religion progressed in an evolutionary fashion from a primitive set of rituals to Christianity, a religion that, these Protestants believed, emphasized good behavior and ethical living. Of course, Wellhausen's interpretation of the Bible was at its core based on supersessionism, an anti-Semitic reading of Judaism as a religious dead end replaced by Christianity, but Kent's and Smith's ideas were widely embraced by modern Protestants in the early twentieth century.

For Snell, recapitulating such themes, the Hebrew Bible illustrated "God's self-revelation in history." He argued that such a story was essential to preserve the faith of young people grappling with the problem of evil; the Bible, he explained, showed how even God's chosen people could only gradually come to full understanding of what God wished for them.[15]

In the spring of 1949, Fielding Smith issued a directive that Snell's book, then available and seeing some use in Church schools for several months, should be used no longer.[16] In March, Snell started an anguished correspondence with Fielding Smith in which he sought to learn why, but also to persuade the inexorable, inflexible Fielding Smith to change his mind. The correspondence did not achieve either of Snell's goals, but it did illustrate Fielding Smith's reasoning.

Fielding Smith barred Snell's book from use for two reasons. The first was obvious; he thought that Snell was simply wrong. He emphasized first to Snell that he believed that correct interpretation of scripture could be achieved only through divine illumination and that therefore the writers Snell leaned on were blinkered. "The sacred writings cannot be interpreted by men who are uninspired," he explained. Such errors led scholars like Snell's teachers to base their interpretation of the Bible on a false premise: that civilization evolved. Fielding Smith denied the premise outright in a letter he sent to Franklin West upon his first encounter with Snell at that January 1937 speech. Snell advocated the "development view of the Hebrew religion," which Fielding Smith believed was easily and simply refuted by scripture itself, if the scholars had eyes to read it.

After all, Fielding Smith explained, in Latter-day Saint scripture the reality of Abraham and Noah was confirmed. "The Lord has revealed to Joseph Smith that Adam and his posterity down to the days of Noah lived," he explained. Latter-day Saint scripture claimed that these figures possessed the fulness of the gospel. What, then, was there to develop? The argument pointed to Fielding Smith's own supersessionism, his belief that the sort of Christianity he himself practiced was eternal, existing from the time of Adam to the present day. He was as convinced as was Snell that Judaism was an anachronism. Talk of development obscured that fact. "The same principles which are given to save us now through the mercy of Jesus Christ were taught to Adam," he claimed. "The Church was organized in the very beginning, and has always been on the earth when an authorized servant clothed in the priesthood could officiate."[17]

But Fielding Smith's objection to Snell went beyond a simple literalism. He was worried about the effects beliefs like Snell's would have both on the Church writ small and society writ large. Another way to put it: Fielding Smith was an intellectual in that he believed ideas had consequences. Beliefs influenced behavior, and modern beliefs would, in his estimation, lead to a broken community. The connection was characteristic of pessimistic anti-moderns; the historian Henry Adams warned of the "mechanical consolidation of force which ruthlessly stamped out" people like Adams himself who did not value an industrial society.[18] Fielding Smith had similar fears.

Snell got at what puzzled the two men about each other in July 1950. In a previous letter to Snell, Fielding Smith had suggested the two personally meet to discuss Snell's book and "let the Standard Works of the Church and the orthodox teachings of the brethren be the measuring rod."[19] The offer illustrated Fielding Smith's presumption that scripture could be read as works of theological orthodoxy, which also characterized the way many conservative Protestants were reading scripture at the time. "The Bible as a whole, taking prophecy and fulfillment together, is the supreme textbook on the subject of faith," wrote J. Gresham Machen, the preeminent theologian of early-twentieth-century Protestant fundamentalism. "The study of that textbook may lead to as clear an understanding of our subject as could be attained." For Machen, the Bible, or, as he asserted, the "whole Bible," indeed could be read as a unified whole, each part (prophecies, for instance) illuminating the other (their fulfillment) and spinning out a coherent systematic theology.[20]

For some Christians, the gap between scripture and theology was so small as to be nonexistent. Machen argued that theology was "just as much a science as is chemistry." He asserted that though theology might be unclear on precise distinctions (as that between, for instance, Calvinists who believed in unconditional predestination and Methodists who did not) the Bible's text taught theology, by which he meant a consistent, clear, and coherent statement of faith. For these Christians, then, the extrapolations of the historic creeds of Christianity were simply restatements of what was already clear in scripture.[21] The same was true for Fielding Smith. For him, the scriptures of the Church always already enunciated what orthodox doctrine should be.

So, when Heber Snell received Fielding Smith's offer to meet, he was confused, and thought he explained why he did little to clarify the disagreement. Snell told Fielding Smith that "the book was not written as theology but as history, and history cannot be cut to fit a theological pattern. History happens and theology can only agree or disagree with it." Thus, he claimed, "the test of orthodoxy is irrelevant in this case," and he chastised Fielding Smith for failing to grasp the fact. "Your error, in my judgment, lies just here: you fail to distinguish between theology and history."[22]

But of course it was not so simple as that. Snell was not simply stating history as it happened; no historian can do that. Rather, his interpretations of the history of Israel reflected the theological liberalism of his teachers and of the sources he drew on. The white, educated liberal Protestants of the early twentieth century distinguished between theology and history by privileging the latter; for them, Christianity properly understood was not primarily doctrinal, but rather, experiential. As Harry Emerson Fosdick, one of the leading liberal Protestants of the age, put it, "In our age especially, we are prone to find God at the end of an argument and leave him there." This was for Fosdick a grievous mistake because, as depicted in the Bible, "experience of the Divine . . . was not dogma. It was life."[23] For liberal Protestants who believed that the Bible revealed the growth of a civilization rather than the enunciation of a theology, experience of the divine was the truth that lay at the end of its pages.

Such were the assumptions Snell brought to the Bible, and his book made it clear that he was being theological while denying theology, interpreting scripture while claiming to simply be doing history. He claimed in the introduction that "The book is not written as sectarian theology but as history," and yet he echoed the theological assumptions of liberal Protestants throughout. "The Jews became engrossed in the means of religion rather than its ends—its theology, ritual and organization, rather than a full morality and depth of spiritual living," Snell wrote, for instance, enunciating a clearly Protestant argument about the meaning and nature of religion entirely in line with that of most Protestant scholars of his time. It was nothing Fosdick would have disputed.[24]

It was the theology that Fielding Smith sniffed out in Snell, and he lambasted it because he believed that its product was more than simply wrong belief it was a fatally weakened society.

Upon reading Snell's book, Fielding Smith peppered the teacher with a series of fourteen questions, "each of which can be answered with a yes or a no." They ranged from catechism—"Do you believe that there was a Garden of Eden?" "Do you believe that Jesus Christ came forth from the dead on the third day after His crucifixion?"- to questions designed to ferret out Snell's allegiance to higher criticism and scholarly analysis of the Bible—"Do you believe that some of the chapters in the Book of Isaiah as we have it in the Bible were written by some other writer than Isaiah?" Smith explained that he was writing in his capacity as chairman of the executive committee of the Church's Board of Education, and that the questions bore on the status of Snell's writings in the Church's educational system.[25]

It was these questions that prompted Snell to protest that his book was not theological and that he did not understand the use of such questions in dealing with a book that he thought to be historical. But for Fielding Smith, theology was inescapable. It bore on how one interpreted scripture, it bore on how one lived one's religion, it bore on how a human society functioned. And, thus, the question of Snell's belief in Jesus's resurrection or the reality of the Garden of Eden was very relevant indeed. "I assure you I have no ill feeling," he told Snell. "But I am greatly concerned over the teachings that are given in the seminaries and institutes in the Church."[26]

As their correspondence continued, Snell offered caveats and clarifications. He remained puzzled about why Fielding Smith took doctrine so seriously, saying that "My view of some questions not (as I believe) of fundamental importance, may differ from that of some writers in the Church. But that fact should not cause a barrier to the book's acceptance." He explained that he believed "the story of the Garden of Eden is intended to symbolize, no doubt, how man 'fell' from his pre-existent, immortal state to mortality." And yet he also affirmed that he believed "Jesus accomplished the atonement and the redemption of man," and that this redemption involved "personal immortality and eternal life." But he stated that he had an "open mind" on whether all the material in the Book of Isaiah was written by Isaiah. And he closed with a restatement of his confusion. "We all see such things according to our study, experience, etc. How could you reasonably expect that I see them precisely as you do?"[27]

Fielding Smith had already made his answer to that question clear. In his letter to Franklin West and Lynn Bennion, the men who ran the Church Education System, he explained that to reject one belief led inevitably to the rejection of another, and another, until ultimately one's faith in God would come crashing down. "If the story of the creation is a mixture of various writers at different times; if the story of the flood is not true; if the story of the Red Sea is a myth, and the Book of Joshua unreliable; moreover if ancient Israel thought they were worshiping the true God, but were not," his litany ran, "then I am left also to conclude that much else that is written is the work of superstitious scribes and uninspired prophets who felt the urge but were not divinely appointed. Where, then, am I to draw the line?"

It seemed nowhere, for no line might hold. After accepting such beliefs, Smith said, "The inspiration of the ancient prophets, therefore, is destroyed." But the march went relentlessly on, because "Jesus in his ministry accepted the story of Jonah and the whale." This was devastating. Jesus was the "Son of God, yet He is just as credulous and subject to these superstitions." And the same was true for Joseph Smith and the Book of Mormon writers. In sum, Fielding Smith said, "with the measuring road of reason and scientific investigation, I find many things which are written by the prophets which we must not accept."[28]

It was for this reason that Fielding Smith believed that incorrect beliefs about the origins of humanity and the earth were such a threat to faith. Here he again revealed his indebtedness to those historians who posited that religion and science were inevitably in conflict, citing figures like John W. Draper not merely as a theorist of the relationship between religion and science but also a victim of their clash. Draper, his fellow historian Andrew Dickson White, and even Charles Darwin all succumbed to the same deadly fall of dominoes. "It is natural for these advocates to deny Adam existed," Fielding Smith observed. He was certain that Darwin's theory made belief in Adam difficult, whatever reconciliations B. H. Roberts might have posited.

"They cannot admit there was an Adam. They must reject the fall and consequently they are forced to reject the atonement of Jesus Christ and his resurrection. It is fatal to their theories to admit any of these things."[29]

But belief in evolution did not merely destroy correct theology; it also encouraged human beings to behave in morally destructive ways. Once human beings lost such confidence in divine revelation and the guidance God offered humanity, Fielding Smith believed they, with their inherent selfishness and moral shortsightedness, would begin building a ruined society. As with many other opponents of the theory of evolution, Fielding Smith did not oppose it merely because he believed it unbiblical; he opposed it because he believed theories of society and history built on the theory of evolution encouraged selfishness and ruthless competition. "Weak nations have had to yield to the strong, who have tried to ease their consciences by the evolutionary doctrine of survival of the fittest," Fielding Smith observed. And the same was true for individuals. The theory of "survival of the fittest" gave some "a code that permitted him to kill his enemy, steal his substance, drive him from his possessions.[30]

He decried the abuse of power, the lack of community, and the moral emptiness he saw in the world around him, and he blamed much of it on a lack of faith. He wrote frankly to his son Douglas, serving in the military in the waning days of World War II that "I believe this struggle over in Europe could have been brought to an end before now and thousands of lives would have been spared if the people in this country, and especially the men in the army, had kept themselves morally clean." And yet the United States was not uniquely at fault. Fielding Smith mourned to his other son, the doomed Lewis, "The people in our own country like those in other lands, have cherished error and tolerated falsehood." Germany had allowed terrible things to occur at the hands of "Hitler, Mussolini, Himler [sic], Goering and the entire mob who have set the world on fire and have murdered, robbed and plundered." Fielding Smith saw the origins of such tragedies in the forgetting of true theology and the embrace of falsehoods like the theory of evolution.[31]

In drawing such connections, Fielding Smith was following the lead of many other conservative Christians in early-twentieth-century America. William Jennings Bryan, the celebrated politician, Presbyterian, and orator, had become friendly with several leaders of the Church in the early 1920s as he stumped the country in opposition to the teaching of evolution in the schools. He delivered his famous lecture series "In His Image" several times in Utah, and Fielding Smith cited Bryan repeatedly in his own work.[32]

In those years, Bryan was becoming among the most vocal and visible of those Christians who called themselves fundamentalists, and he warned repeatedly that a loss of faith in God would inevitably lead to social decay. An ardent advocate for redistribution of wealth and pacifism, Bryan blamed the theory of evolution for the violence of the twentieth-century world. Like Fielding Smith, Bryan assumed that belief in evolution would lead to belief in social evolution; that the principle of change over time would lead people to the conclusion that progress came only through struggle, and that there-fore only those who successfully struggled deserved progress. For William Jennings Bryan, looking at the world of World War I and gross exploitation of the working classes, the principle was obvious. "The brute doctrine of the survival of the fittest is driving men into a life-or-death struggle from which sympathy and the spirit of brotherhood are eliminated," he declared in "In His Image." "It is transforming the industrial world into a slaughterhouse." For Bryan, "the bloodiest war in history would seem enough to condemn Darwinism," but he also laid at its feet the rise of industrial capitalism, the struggle of the wealthy to get greater gain at the expense of the weaker, and the language of merit and hard work that justified it.[33]

For all these reasons, Fielding Smith worried that, if Heber Snell were allowed to continue teaching, he, and those like him, would destroy the Church of Jesus Christ of Latter-day Saints.

He told Snell this frankly. When Snell proposed—with heartbreaking idealism, and perhaps naïveté—that Fielding Smith and himself engage in a debate of open letters in the Church newspaper the *Deseret News*, Fielding Smith dismissed any sort of "public discussion in the press which would serve only further to spread the erroneous ideas carried in your book." Instead, Fielding Smith offered to "sit down with you anytime personally." The aim, however, would not be a discussion leading to exchange and compromise but rather simply to "correct errors."[34]

Joseph Fielding Smith and the Intellectuals

So Snell accepted. He had little other choice and was growing desperate for both recognition of his work and preservation of his career. He sent a flurry of letters to other General Authorities of the Church pleading for positive feedback on his book; he often received gentle, bemused answers that did little to help his cause. In January 1950, he was informed that his contract at the Institute of Religion in Logan, Utah, would not be renewed—which might have been due to his age (by then, sixty-seven) or to his collision with Fielding Smith.[35]

With all these worries on him, Snell visited Fielding Smith at his office in Salt Lake City on Wednesday August 23, 1950. Fielding Smith invited two other general authorities of the church and protégés of his, Harold B. Lee and Marion Romney. He had suggested Snell bring two friends also; Snell misunderstood whom Fielding Smith suggested (two church officials who liked Snell) and ended up bringing his wife and his friend Sterling McMurrin. A former teacher in the Church's institutes program himself, McMurrin was by 1950 a professor of philosophy at the University of Utah with a national reputation. He would eventually serve as the chief of education in John F. Kennedy's presidential administration. McMurrin had also read drafts of Snell's book and wrote a preface for it.[36]

The Snell controversy was followed soon by the publication of *Man: His Origin and Destiny,* Fielding Smith's most controversial book and, between the two events, Fielding Smith would find himself taking a number of meetings with scholars like Snell and McMurrin through the 1950s. His reputation among the intellectual community in the Church began to decline in that decade, as did his own sense that he was defending the Church against those who would attempt to flatten its particularity and degrade the specifics of its doctrine. Other than Snell, McMurrin was the first to report on the intransigence of Fielding Smith, making him into the symbol of doctrinal enforcement that he became by his death. Fielding Smith became that symbol in part because those who engaged with him later in his life were sympathetic to liberal Protestant ideals that downplayed and rejected doctrine as a valuable measure of religious orthodoxy. McMurrin's report of his encounter with Fielding Smith is a case in point.

Snell reported that he was surprised by Fielding Smith's "kindness, you know, his decency." Fielding Smith insisted on reimbursing Snell for his travel to Salt Lake, taking a ten-dollar bill from his own pocket and pressing it on Snell. He also said that Fielding Smith "never thought of calling me down by authority"; the apostle did not spend the meeting berating Snell. But he was firm.[37]

McMurrin recorded a description of the encounter for transcription. He reported the meeting lasted all morning, breaking up only when the apostles had to leave to attend a funeral, and that the major discussants were Snell, Fielding Smith, Harold B. Lee, and McMurrin himself. McMurrin, in his recollections, made two primary points about Fielding Smith. On the one hand, he said, he was alarmed "to see what extent he simply was completely uninformed about the Bible." On the other hand, he conceded, "He was quite adept at making references to the Bible in connection with Mormon doctrine." Snell, McMurrin said, was "a scholar who was accustomed to a careful consideration of evidence and knew a great deal about the subject. Fielding Smith, McMurrin said, "was essentially a dogmatist [who] knew the answers and knew in advance that everything else, in a sense, had to be thrown out."[38]

The meeting revealed less Fielding Smith's ignorance about the Bible than a fundamental distinction between what McMurrin and Snell conceived to be the meaning and importance of religion and how Fielding Smith thought about the same questions.

The two academics were baffled by the apostle's seeming misunderstanding of the purpose behind Snell's book. At one point, McMurrin remembered, Fielding Smith was worrying that Snell "didn't bring religion into the book." McMurrin broke in to reiterate a point Snell himself had made in his letters to Fielding Smith. "The book has religion in it from beginning to end," he told the apostle. "The history of Israel, ancient Israel, is the story of a special revelation from God to man." That Fielding Smith did not agree with that reading revealed to McMurrin that the "man was blind to the kind of thing that Snell was doing."[39]

But Fielding Smith was not blind. He just disagreed with the premise. He told McMurrin in response that the professor was speaking "as if there was a kind of historical development of the conception of God among these people in the Old Testament." Well, of course, McMurrin said. "It's in his book because it's in the Bible." He then said that the apostle was simply restating "the old anti-historical approach to the history of religion." And there the two left it. McMurrin had put his finger precisely on what Fielding Smith was arguing, but he seemed more able to dismiss the idea than engage with it.[40]

For Snell and McMurrin, the religion of the Bible was the story of progression they assumed lay in its pages. But their reading of the Bible was not simply axiomatic. For Fielding Smith, religion was not a story of progress. Rather, the religion he expected to see in the book was the presence of the clear and consistent doctrine of the Church of Jesus Christ of Latter-day Saints he believed was present from the time of Adam and Eve until the present day. The concern he had with Snell's book—and with McMurrin's ideas—was that they did not interpret the history of religion in such a way as to emphasize the clarity of doctrine.

As McMurrin predicted, the meeting got Snell nowhere. He had told Snell that Fielding Smith "wasn't reasonable at all," by which McMurrin meant the apostle was not a liberal in the same way he thought Snell was a liberal, somebody who "really believed in the rationality of the human race."[41] Snell thought that if he could simply phrase his case in the right way, Fielding Smith would realize his book was in fact excellent. McMurrin, even though he did not seem himself to quite grasp where Fielding Smith was coming from, knew better. The meeting changed nothing about Snell's fate or the fate of his book.

But it did lead to further dialogue between the apostle and the professor. Soon after the meeting with Snell, Fielding Smith reached out to McMurrin asking for another meeting, without Snell this time. It took a while to coordinate schedules and it was nearly a year before McMurrin returned to Fielding Smith's office, met again by the apostle and his younger colleague Harold B. Lee. In total, Fielding Smith and McMurrin met three times between 1950 and 1954 and, according to McMurrin, the apostles wanted to talk theology; about, as Lee told him, "what it is you personally believe."[42]

The first meeting after the discussion over Snell's book was much taken up with conversation about a discussion group that McMurrin helped to run at the University of Utah colloquially called the "Swearing Elders." The group consisted of academics interested in discussing intellectual problems with relation to the Church. Fielding Smith had caught wind of it and McMurrin explained that the apostle was often criticized in these meetings for his "writings in theology and history, and especially theology." He told Fielding Smith that his critics at least paid him the compliment of "saying what you honestly believe, even though they think some of the things you say are ridiculous." Fielding Smith apparently "smiled" at this. Then McMurrin gave him an example. In a recent speech, McMurrin paraphrased Fielding Smith as stating that "the negroes are getting exactly what they deserve."[43]

84

At this point, Fielding Smith broke in and asked McMurrin, "Let me tell you what I think." He then reiterated the racist conclusions he had written in many, many texts by that point, overriding McMurrin's explanation that many of those in the "Swearing Elders," supporters of civil rights, were uncomfortable with Fielding Smith's conclusions. To Fielding Smith, the doctrine as he understood it trumped such transient concerns, and he was made only more determined at the news that he faced resistance. He told McMurrin that he had no wish for the meetings to end. He said he simply asked that McMurrin, at the end of each meeting, "give them the position of the Church, so they fully understand what the Church's position is."[44] Ironically sounding a bit like Snell, Fielding Smith seemed to believe that clear presentation of theology would clear up disagreement.

In this meeting and their next and last, Fielding Smith explained to McMurrin that he bore the professor no ill will. McMurrin noted that Fielding Smith scrupulously addressed him as "Dr. McMurrin," never raised his voice, and went out of his way to express concern for McMurrin's personal well-being and family. And yet, McMurrin noted, Fielding Smith repeatedly and consistently used phrases like "refusing to believe in the doctrine," "departing from the doctrine," and, of course, the word *orthodox*.[45]

For McMurrin himself, a liberal Protestant at heart, such a premise was questionable. "The Church as an institution does not have a serious, honest interest in the scholarly study of religion or in a genuinely authentic search for truth," he mused, thinking about the sorts of questions Fielding Smith pressed him on. Because of McMurrin's philosophical commitments, for him authenticity and orthodoxy lay at odds with each other. But for Fielding Smith, precision in doctrine was the beating heart of a real and vibrant religious community. His questions to McMurrin made it clear. As he had with Snell, Fielding Smith wanted to know whether McMurrin believed in the reality of the fall of Adam and Eve, the truth of Jesus Christ's death and resurrection, and the power of the atonement Jesus accomplished. McMurrin demurred on each. In particular, he rejected the notion of the fall as "a vicious thing." Human beings, McMurrin believed, were basically positive and human history, in his opinion, revealed progress rather than stagnation in sin. He found Jesus to be a great and wise teacher, but not divine.[46]

A few months later McMurrin learned that members of his own congregation, worried about his orthodoxy, had met with Fielding Smith. They claimed the apostle said McMurrin "should be excommunicated from the Church and that efforts were being made to have this done." All this, of course, smelled of gossip, and McMurrin noted the report seemed garbled. But Fielding Smith's intent seemed clear. After all, Fielding Smith did at the same time have one of McMurrin's friends and ideological sympathizers, George Boyd, removed from his teaching position in the Church. In a later account, McMurrin claimed he went to David O. McKay, then president of the Church, who made clear he would intervene on McMurrin's behalf in any excommunication process.[47]

No such procedure ever went forward. But the story spread, and it was becoming clear to many in the Church that Fielding Smith had come to consider himself an advocate for doctrinal orthodoxy willing to defend that orthodoxy if necessary. He also seemed to grow colder toward McMurrin. In 1960, a young man named Fred Morrison wrote to Fielding Smith complaining that McMurrin was still a member of the Church. The professor was "a member in name only," and, in classes Morrison took from him at the University of Utah, McMurrin made it clear he "sees no saving virtues in any of the principles of the restored Gospel." Morrison demanded, "Why is this man not excommunicated from the Church?"[48]

Fielding Smith's response was exact, echoing the same concerns he had expressed to Snell. He told Morrison he believed that doctrinal rigor and orthodoxy was of particular concern among educators. Because of his twin statuses as unorthodox and a teacher of the young, therefore, Fielding Smith stated bluntly that "Sterling M. McMurrin is a betrayer of the Church." Yet that was not enough. "There is nothing I can do about it," he told Morrison. "Why not present your case to the First Presidency?" Fielding Smith's response indicates McMurrin's belief that McKay was protecting him might have had some weight.[49]

At roughly the same time, Fielding Smith had encounters with two other prominent LDS intellectuals, the chemist Henry Eyring and the historian Richard Poll. Both interactions could be ultimately traced to the publication of *Man: His Origin and Destiny* in 1954. Eyring, a nationally respected scientist who had taught at Princeton for years, was quite uncomfortable with the book's treatment of science. Poll was one of the participants in the Swearing Elders group, which spent several sessions discussing the book and Fielding Smith's conservative theology. The two engaged with Fielding Smith along different routes, and their encounters differed in concern and tone, and yet the apostle took a position similar to the one he took with McMurrin. He insisted that orthodox belief was necessary for the preservation of a genuine religious faith.

Fielding Smith wrote to Poll, a professor at BYU, on December 1, 1954, soon after his meetings with McMurrin. He said he had "been informed" Poll attended the Swearing Elders group a few weeks before, when *Man: His Origin and Destiny* was criticized, and wanted to know whether Poll was "properly quoted." He did not elaborate on what he believed Poll had said. The two had a short exchange of letters, and Fielding Smith invited Poll to his office for a discussion. "I would be happy to see you personally," he said, "and perhaps we can get a little nearer in our views."[50]

Poll and his wife visited Church headquarters on December 29. They briefly conferred with David O. McKay, president of the Church, before walking down the hall to Fielding Smith's office. McKay assured them that, as far as he was concerned, Fielding Smith's "book is not the authoritative position of the Church." When they reached Fielding Smith's office, Poll explained to Smith that he was one of "a large number of teachers in the Church who do not denounce or debunk" Fielding Smith's ideas, but regardless "do not find it possible to accept all the doctrines which Brother Smith presents as fundamental." Poll wanted to know whether such people could have a home in the church. Like McMurrin, he presented to Fielding Smith the image of a church built not on doctrinal uniformity but on willing participation despite holding a range of theological positions. As he wrote in response to Fielding Smith's December 1 letter, though he respected Fielding Smith's beliefs, "I fervently hope that comparable conviction is not to be required of all Latter-day Saints in the days to come."[51]

In the same weeks he was engaging with Poll, Fielding Smith was also dealing with Henry Eyring. On December 16, 1954, Eyring wrote a letter to the apostle Adam Bennion, who had asked for the chemist's opinion on *Man: His Origin and Destiny*. Both Eyring and Bennion seemed to believe the letter would be widely circulated, and Eyring took care not only to thoroughly explore the scientific evidence that placed "the beginning of life on this earth back at about one billion years" but also to express his deep affection for Fielding Smith as a religious leader. The book was "the work of a great man who is fallible," Eyring wrote. Church leaders "have been given to understand clearly the road we should follow and can point the path to the celestial kingdom, but being human they too must walk by faith" in many other areas. Eyring made a distinction between religion and science that worried Fielding Smith, who believed, from his reading of scholars like Andrew Dickson White, that such a clear distinction was an ideological strategy destined to destroy religion.[52]

Fielding Smith sent Eyring a reply. Indeed, he had engaged with Eyring before. Four years earlier, Fielding Smith had sent Eyring a long letter commenting on his worry about some materials Eyring and other Church scientists had prepared for the youth curriculum.[53] But, despite the length of time between the two encounters, his responses to Eyring and to Poll show a consistent outlook.

First, Fielding Smith felt under siege. He wrote to Eyring that scholars often held religious people in contempt. "We who believe in the mission of Jesus Christ have been designated as curs; our doctrine ridiculed," he said. "We have been designated as ignorant, harking back to the days of 'primitive savagery and ignorance,' for believing the foolish doctrine of an anthropomorphic God!"[54] He perceived himself as he perceived his ancestors, standing for truth against a world that seemed determined to destroy it. He did not perceive the theory of evolution as a simple value-neutral statement about the work of the world; rather, it seemed to him a deliberate conspiracy, formed specifically for the destruction of religious faith. He said as much to both Poll and Eyring, explaining to the former his concern "over the problem of evolutionist teaching and its effect on testimony."[55]

Second, Fielding Smith was utterly convinced that only by holding closely to theology could the community of his Church be saved. He clarified the position he had come to in his debates with Heber Snell for Eyring and Poll, telling the latter that the spread of belief in evolution would enable those who sought to "ridicule the Scripture and undermine confidence in the Church." He warned Eyring that those who held to "any theory which is in conflict with the revelations given by the Lord . . . will perish."[56]

But, finally, Fielding Smith exhibited less certainty when he grappled with the position of both Poll and Eyring, men who assured him that they simultaneously held to belief in the atonement of Jesus Christ and faith in the church and yet questioned the apostle's firm and specific theology. Both Poll and Eyring leaned on the work of James Talmage and John Widtsoe, apostles who had evidenced sympathy for scientific findings about the age of the earth. Fielding Smith told Poll that he had good "awareness of the size of this group" and that he "did not think they should be excommunicated or barred from teaching." Poll expressed hope for "peaceful coexistence," noting Fielding Smith did not seem entirely triumphant. "President Smith was quite as concerned about justifying his own position as about criticizing ours," he observed.[57]

With these men, Fielding Smith seemed more conciliatory than he did with figures like McMurrin or Snell, and the difference seemed to lie in his own psychology as much as in his doctrine. Despite the aggressiveness in Fielding Smith's rhetoric, Poll had put his finger on what was behind it. From the time he was a small boy, Fielding Smith had felt under threat. He sought sympathy almost as much as he did converts.

Heirs

By the time of the Church's semiannual General Conference of April 1975, Fielding Smith had been dead for nearly three years. But his influence hung over the proceedings.

On Saturday morning, in the first session of the conference, William Grant Bangerter, an assistant to the Quorum of the Twelve Apostles, recounted a conversation he had had when he received a call from the apostle Mark Petersen, who wanted Bangerter to serve as a stake president, presiding over a number of local congregations in Salt Lake City.

"'Brother Bangerter, do you believe in the gospel?" Petersen asked.

I responded that I did insofar as I understood it.

He said, 'No, I mean do you believe in the gospel according to Joseph Fielding Smith?'"

Bangerter said he recounted this story to drive home the point that "Because of the strictness with which President Smith taught the doctrines of the gospel, this was a story that could separate the sheep from the goats."[58]

Though Fielding Smith was dead, Bangerter's honoring of his legacy showed that not only did particular ideas the old theologian taught survive him—opposition to the theory of evolution, insistence on an earth not more than a few thousand years old—but so did his particular orientation to ideas. For Bangerter and Petersen, it was not simply belief in any single ideas that might mark one a sheep; it was fidelity to the idea that doctrine itself was significant and that believing in the doctrine as taught by Joseph Fielding Smith was a mark of the true faith.

In that same General Conference of the Church, a few hours after Bangerter, the apostle Bruce R. McConkie spoke. Fielding Smith's son-in-law, husband to his daughter Amelia, McConkie had with his father-in-law's blessing taken up his mantle as the Church's great advocate for rigor and purity in theology. He had ascended to the Quorum of the Twelve Apostles upon Fielding Smith's death in July 1972. That April, McConkie urged members of the Church to "consecrate a portion of our time to systematic study, to becoming gospel scholars, to treasuring up the revealed truths which guide us in paths of truth and righteousness."[59]

In so doing, he was, he believed, fulfilling the legacy of his father-in-law. When Fielding Smith became president of the church in 1970, McConkie declared, "Our new president is a doctrinal teacher, a theologian, a scriptorian, a preacher of righteousness in the full and true sense of the word." It was, McConkie said, the "final gospel dispensation" and he suggested it was "of necessity" that a man like Fielding Smith lead the Church at the time.[60] Certainly, Fielding Smith believed it.

In the end, there are at least two ways we might read Fielding Smith. One is to see him as a somewhat prescient critic of the liberal Protestant, progressive vision of civilization, a vision that encouraged antisemitism in Wellhausen and supersessionism in others, a vision that encouraged imperialism and colonialism. Julius Wellhausen's understanding of ancient Israel has been roundly criticized; as Jon Levenson points out, Wellhausen's presumption that ritualism is a sign of a civilization's late paralysis seems now neither philosophically nor historically correct. Fielding Smith was probably right to reject the hypothesis.

Fielding Smith's suspicion of progress found good company with other antimodernists like Henry Adams and some Protestant fundamentalists or even neoorthodox theologians. But while, on some level, such comparisons are illuminating, it is probably also fair to say that Fielding Smith was right for the wrong reasons. Though his understanding of race emphasized stasis rather than progress, he was no less a believer that people with different skin colors had different spiritual, mental, and intellectual capacities than did his fellow Anglo-Saxons. Similarly, though he may have been correct to reject the oversimplified, Protestant-centric reading of the Bible Snell and McMurrin offered him, Fielding Smith's own interpretations of the text were equally marked by culture-bound assumptions he did not recognize.

His tendency to use words like *plain* to describe the Bible and various LDS scripture revealed the marks of Protestant fundamentalist particulars as much as their deeper inclinations toward antimodernism. He was just as racist in his own ways as those he critiqued.

In the end, Fielding Smith is something of a mystery; a *sui generis* thinker in his own generation who became the model theologian for many after him; one definitely suspicious of the intellectual establishment of his day whose thought was as complex and comprehensive as theirs; a pessimist in a time of optimism. And yet, to understand the history not simply of the Church of Jesus Christ of Latter-day Saints in the twentieth century but of the emergence of conservative religion in the United States and beyond, Fielding Smith, and those like him, must be taken seriously. Not simply throwbacks or cranks, they are modern people in their own way and thus reveal the composite and contradictory nature of the world they have left to us.

Bibliographic Essay

Joseph Fielding Smith was, in his own way, a polymath. Though he had very little formal education, he did not hesitate to write about things important to him. His work, while all dealing with religion, ranges across the fields of history and science and biblical criticism. Some are classic nineteenth-century pamphlet polemics; others are long, deeply researched theses. It is possible to clump his twenty-five books and pamphlets, and his many articles into genres, and some scholars have, dividing his works into studies of history, theology, and compilations of his sermons and other writings.[1] Here I will group his work into two primary categories—history and theology—paying attention to the evolution of Fielding Smith's thought over his career.

His first published work was the 1902 article "Asahel Smith of Topsfield, with Some Account of the Smith Family," which appeared in the *Historical Collections of the Topsfield Historical Society*.[2] It was one of only two pieces he published in his life in a venue intended for a non-Latter-day Saint audience. (The other was a brief survey of the history of the Church, "The Hundredth Anniversary of the Mormon Church," published in 1930 in *Arrowhead* magazine.[3]) But even in the forementioned piece, Fielding Smith's concerns were evident. He praised Asahel's faithfulness to Christianity, emphasized that the Smith family was "guided through the inspiration of the Lord," and closed with a discussion of Joseph Smith Jr.'s work in founding the Church of Jesus Christ of Latter-day Saints.[4]

For a time, history remained Fielding Smith's primary interest, even as he sharpened his conviction that history was properly interpreted as a revelation of divine intentions rather than a record of human activity.

Many of the publications he produced immediately after "Asahel Smith of Topsfield" contributed to his sparring with Richard Evans of the Reorganized Church of Jesus Christ of Latter-day Saints in the first decade of the twentieth century. *Blood Atonement and the Origins of Plural Marriage* (1905), *The "Reorganized" Church vs. Salvation for the Dead* (1905), and *Origin of the "Reorganized" Church and the Question of Succession* (1907) all sought to defend the historical claims of the LDS Church and debunk those of the Reorganized Church of Jesus Christ of Latter-day Saints. He focused on three particular questions—the origins of LDS temple rituals, including baptism for the dead; the authority of the Quorum of the Twelve Apostles, which had assumed leadership of the LDS Church after the death of Joseph Smith; and the reality of Joseph Smith's practice of polygamy, which the RLDS Church sought to delegitimize.[5]

In each pamphlet, Fielding Smith made twin arguments. The first was historical. Fielding Smith adeptly mustered affidavits, primary sources, and letters to assail RLDS claims. He pointed out Evans's use of incomplete quotations; he cited documents left by a number of women who claimed to have been married to Joseph Smith Jr. polygamously; he recounted the apparently chaotic origins of the RLDS Church. In all this he proved himself a competent master of the tools of the historical trade.[6]

The second style of argument he levied showed his confidence that history and scripture were equally useful and applicable sources of authority. He argued that the RLDS were incorrect in their rejection of polygamy by reference to the Book of Genesis. He maintained that, as the revelations of Joseph Smith provided the procedure for ordination to office, it was possible to judge which ordinations were proper by virtue of measuring them against that scripture. He compared Brigham Young's behavior with that of Book of Mormon figures to demonstrate that Young acted as a prophet should. In short, he looked to scripture to see how God would guide human history and then measured the history of his church against that model. It set the patterns for his larger and fuller works of history that would follow.[7]

The major works of theological history to which I allude are *Essentials in Church History* (1922), *The Way to Perfection* (1931), *The Progress of Man* (1936), *Life of Joseph F. Smith: Sixth President of the Church of Jesus Christ of Latter-day Saints* (1938), *The Signs of the Times* (1942), and *Church History and Modern Revelation* (1946–49).

The narrative histories among them—*Essentials in Church History, Life of Joseph F. Smith,* and *Church History and Modern Revelation*—present the story of the LDS Church as Fielding Smith understood it. The first and third were intended as manuals of study for gatherings of the Church. The first is a single volume, and the last is a multivolume exploration of many of the same themes, emphasizing God's revelation to and guidance of the Church. All the volumes build on a long legacy, running back to nineteenth-century Church historians like George A. Smith, George Q. Cannon, and Joseph Smith himself, of presenting the history of the Church as a combination of ruthless persecution driven by falsehoods and evildoers but simultaneously guided by God. Moreover, they contextualize the history of the LDS Church not in the contours of US history, but rather in the broader, and even cosmic, narrative of the Bible and other Latter-day Saint scripture. Thus, *Essentials in Church History* begins not with Joseph Smith but in a preexistent time when God determined to create the earth and extends through the temporal existence of the Church on earth. *Life of Joseph F. Smith* begins with the origins of the Smith family itself, emphasizing Joseph Smith Jr. and Joseph F.'s father Hyrum. The first paints the history of the Church as a long series of obstacles overcome through devotion to God and subsequent divine guidance; the latter presents that same story in miniature, depicting Joseph Fielding Smith's father as a righteous man constantly beset by adversaries, from those who killed his father to hostile senators interrogating him before Congress, just as his own ancestors were.[8]

The Way to Perfection, The Progress of Man, and *The Signs of the Times* reach more broadly in their scope than do the works on LDS history. These three present themselves as sweeping stories of the entire human race, the first two from human preexistence to the present time and the last as the story of the future—from the current time to the coming of Jesus Christ. In this they are salvation histories, a long-standing Christian genre that take its model from the Bible itself. They show how Fielding Smith could rely equally on traditional historical documentation and on the sacred stories of scripture. The first gave him facts and particulars, but the second gave him structure and rules. He consistently filtered the first through the second and sought to show how the story of humanity was, in a sense, predetermined by the history of salvation first and foremost.

The Way to Perfection and *The Progress of Man* are unofficial companion volumes.[9] The first, written for the Genealogical Society of Utah as a guide intended to spur more people to do the work of family history and proxy ordinances for those whom research uncovered, surveyed the story of human creation and of God's plan of salvation. It explained the history of what Fielding Smith believed to be the true church of God throughout the human past, retelling the stories of the Bible and the Book of Mormon and weaving particularly LDS themes like priesthood and temples into those familiar stories. *The Progress of Man* tells, in a sense, the same story again but emphasizes what might be called secular history. Here, Fielding Smith emphasizes the history of nations, government, and culture. The story he tells is a fairly conventional recounting of "Western" history, a genre just then emerging in US schools and universities, and he draws on conventional histories to tell it rather than on any sort of primary research. The book traces human civilization from the Middle East through Europe to the United States, emphasizing the hand-in-hand emergence of Protestantism and democracy. But while many conventional histories framed the story as one of human accomplishment, Fielding Smith instead tells it as the story of God's work in preparing the world for the restoration of the true church. The Reformation and Renaissance thus he paints as inspired by God but also afflicted with human errors; the American Revolution and the Enlightenment are treated similarly. The story told here is therefore ambivalent, emphasizing divine rather than human agency. It is in these books that Fielding Smith's ideas about lineage and race receive their fullest exploration.

In contrast, *The Signs of the Times* is a dispensationalist plotting of the future of human civilization, telling the story of the Second Coming of Jesus Christ and the various tragedies and disasters that Fielding Smith expected would precede it.[10] The book began life as a series of lectures delivered in the fall of 1942 at the Lion House, the historic home of Brigham Young functioning then as a social club, and it is very much a work of the World War II period. Fielding Smith's tone in the original lectures is pessimistic and grim. He guardedly speculates that Adolf Hitler is the Antichrist. The creation of a Jewish homeland lifted his spirits and prompted him to revisit and expand the original six lectures after the end of the war and the proclamation of the state of Israel in 1948. Here, Fielding Smith's tone is one of guarded optimism for Christ's return. Through much of the book Fielding

Smith proof texts the Bible and Doctrine and Covenants, weaving together a story of tribulation and Second Coming.

The crowning achievement of Fielding Smith's work as a theologian is *Man: His Origin and Destiny* (1954).[11] The book emerged from the materials Smith prepared to rebut B. H. Roberts's attempt to reconcile the theories of evolution and an ancient earth in the early 1930s. By the early 1950s, the members of the First Presidency who had issued a moratorium on the debate between Smith and Roberts and two of the scientists who had served as apostles during the controversy, James Talmage and John Widtsoe, were all dead. Smith reworked his materials and released them in a massive, 563-page volume. The book spent five chapters painstakingly rebutting what Fielding Smith called "the hypothesis of organic evolution," and another three assailing academic criticism of the Bible, defending the reliability of scripture as a source for the history of humanity. In the third chapter of the book, Smith insisted that "All truth *is* dogmatic." He meant by this that certain religious assertions of Christianity, the story of humanity's salvation Fielding Smith had told before, the special creation of Adam and Eve, the fall of humanity, and the coming, death, and resurrection of Jesus Christ, could be treated as revealed and settled fact, belief in which was essential to be a faithful Christian. To that he added particular assertions of the Latter-day Saint restoration: the special calling of Joseph Smith, the reality of priesthood, and the authority of LDS sacraments.[12] In 1954, Smith and apostle Harold B. Lee assigned the book to the secondary teachers the Church employed, and it gained a strong following in the Church Education System in the decades that followed.

Fielding Smith's other works of pure theology were smaller in scale than the massive achievement of *Man: His Origin and Destiny*. Earlier in his life, as part of his advocacy for the Genealogical Society of Utah, he produced two small pamphlets, *Elijah the Prophet and His Mission* (1924) and *Salvation Universal* (1912).[13] The latter pamphlet made the argument that Latter-day Saint belief in proxy sacraments for the dead made his church the only real believers in universal salvation on the face of the earth. He particularly assailed Protestants who disparaged sacramental faiths for being exclusive, arguing that their belief in salvation through faith alone rendered helpless the many human beings who never heard the name of Jesus Christ. The former pamphlet focused on the Hebrew prophet Elijah, who, in Latter-day Saint belief, held the authority to bind together the generations.

Toward the end of his life, Fielding Smith released two volumes of compiled sermons and religious writings, *Take Heed to Yourselves* (1966) and *Seek Ye Earnestly* (1970). Both were edited by his son, Joseph Fielding Smith Jr. The first compilation targeted the theme of repentance; the second, appropriately, counseled Church members to study scripture and develop their knowledge of the theology of their faith. While most of the sermons in both volumes were those given at major Church events, like the biannual General Conferences, both volumes included material most Church members would not have had access to—addresses given in Fielding Smith's own local congregation, for instance, and other speeches in smaller venues.[14]

Despite his multitude of other writings, it is likely most Latter-day Saints encountered Joseph Fielding Smith's work in one of the compilations he is most famous for: the five-volume *Answers to Gospel Questions* (1957–66), edited by his son, Joseph Fielding Smith Jr., or the three volumes of *Doctrines of Salvation* (1954–56), edited by Bruce R. McConkie, Fielding Smith's son-in-law.[15] *Answers to Gospel Questions* gathered together more than two hundred fifty of the questions Fielding Smith had received from members of the Church over more than twenty years, together with his short answers to questions as far-flung as "Why did Jesus come alive again?" and whether Ouija boards were evil.[16] In *Doctrines of Salvation*, McConkie organized a vast corpus of Fielding Smith's sermons and extracts from his published books, newspaper columns, and other shorter writings into an encyclopedic selection of themes—ranging from the cosmic implications of "The Character, Attributes, and Perfection of God" opening the first volume to the far more tangible "The Mormon Pioneers and Colonization" closing the third. Between them, the two volumes were among the first presentations of a theology of the Latter-day Saints systematically and thoroughly presented.

McConkie and Fielding Smith Jr., intended the volumes not only to celebrate and extend the influence of Fielding Smith, which they accomplished but also to mirror Fielding Smith's own work in the influential 1938 compilation *The Teachings of the Prophet Joseph Smith*.[17] Much as his own editors took Fielding Smith's work and transformed it into a comprehensive understanding of the world for the members of their church, in his volume, Fielding Smith sought to highlight the ideas and words of his ancestor that had not been canonized, making the thoughts of Joseph Smith Jr. far more widely available and, hence, Fielding Smith hoped, influential. As he wrote, perhaps aspirationally, in the volume's introduction, "The members of the Church quite generally desire to know what the Prophet Joseph Smith may have said on important subjects, for they look upon his utterances as coming through divine inspiration."[18] He relied primarily on sermons published in early Latter-day Saint newspapers and compiled in the official history of the Church, and on his assistants in the Church Historian's Office.

The 1938 compilation, and those his son and son-in-law produced, were efforts to achieve what Fielding Smith hoped to accomplish his entire life: produce a theology, and even a dogma, out of Latter-day Saint scripture. He wrote so much because he believed ideas were essential, and that his faith's strength lay in its ideas. And by the time of his death, he had imprinted that conviction on his church.

Notes

Chapter 1. An Intellectual Life

1. Joseph Fielding Smith's reminiscence excerpted from Joseph Fielding Smith Jr. and John Stewart, *The Life of Joseph Fielding Smith* (Salt Lake City: Deseret, 1972), 38.

2. Joseph Fielding Smith, *The Life of Joseph F. Smith, Sixth President of the Church of Jesus Christ of Latter-day Saints* (Salt Lake City: Deseret, 1938), 282.

3. Bruce R. McConkie, "Joseph Fielding Smith, Apostle, Prophet, Father in Israel," *Ensign*, August 1972, 25.

4. Both Smith and Stewart, *Life of Joseph Fielding Smith*, 89–90, and Francis M. Gibbons, *Joseph Fielding Smith: Gospel Scholar, Prophet of God* (Salt Lake City: Deseret, 1992), 71, had access to Fielding Smith's journals and quote from them.

5. Joseph F. McConkie, *True and Faithful: The Life Story of Joseph Fielding Smith* (Salt Lake City: Bookcraft, 1971), 26. This book is by Fielding Smith's grandson, who used his grandfather's personal papers and recordings to construct the biography.

6. Smith and Stewart, *Life of Joseph Fielding Smith*, 91.

7. Joseph Fielding Smith to Rachel Smith, January 30, 1900, MS 3300, Church of Jesus Christ of Latter-day Saints History Library and Archives, Salt Lake City, Utah. Hereafter Church History Library and Archives.

8. Smith and Stewart, *Life of Joseph Fielding Smith*, 39.

9. Smith, *Life of Joseph F. Smith*, 4, 404.

10. Joseph' Fielding Smith, "Asahel Smith of Topsfield, with Some Account of the Smith Family," *Historical Collections of the Topsfield Historical Society* 8 (1902): 87–101.

11. Joseph Fielding Smith to Joseph F. Smith, October 24, 1909, Joseph F. Smith Papers, MS 1325, Church History Library and Archives.

12. James B. Allen, Jessie Embry, and Kahlil Mehr, *Hearts Turned to the Fathers: A History of the Genealogical Society of Utah* (Provo, UT: BYU Studies Press, 1995), 71–76.

13. Joseph Fielding Smith to Sterling Sill, no date, box 34, folder 7, Sterling W. Sill Papers, Special Collections, J. Willard Marriott Library, University of Utah. Hereafter Marriott Library Special Collections.

14. McConkie, *True and Faithful*, 99.

15. His first patriarchal blessing is transcribed in part in Smith and Stewart, *Life of Joseph Fielding Smith*, 49–50; a copy of the second is in box 10, folder 13, David Buerger Papers, Marriott Library Special Collections.

16. Smith and Stewart, *Life of Joseph Fielding Smith,* 170.

17. Quoted in Smith and Stewart, *Life of Joseph Fielding Smith*, 169.

18. Gibbons, *Joseph Fielding Smith*, 226–36. For Fielding Smith's enthusiasm for collegiate football, see, for example, Joseph Fielding Smith to Lewis Smith, October 29, 1944, Joseph Fielding Smith Family Correspondence, MS 14132, Church History Library and Archives.

19. Smith and Stewart, *Life of Joseph Fielding Smith*, 242, 249.

20. The stories are drawn from Linda Harris, "The Legend of Jessie Evans Smith," *Utah Historical Quarterly* 44, no. 4 (1976): 315–64; Fielding Smith and Jessie banter about the piano and other things in "Joseph Fielding Smith Interview, ca 1971," MS 5288, Church History Library and Archives.

21. Joseph Fielding Smith to Douglas Smith, February 17, 1945, and February 9, 1945. Joseph Fielding Smith Family Correspondence, MS14132, Church History Library and Archives.

22. Joseph Fielding Smith to Douglas Smith, May 22, 1945, Joseph Fielding Smith Family Correspondence, MS14132, Church History Library and Archives.

23. Leonard Arrington, "Joseph Fielding Smith: Faithful Historian," *Dialogue* 7, no. 1 (Spring 1972): 21–24.

24. On the rise of higher education and its transformation of knowledge in the United States, see George Marsden, *The Soul of the American University Revisited: From Protestant to Postsecular* (New York: Oxford University Press, 2021), 89–151; Julie Ruben, *The Making of the Modern University: Intellectual Transformation and the Marginalization of Morality* (Chicago: University of Chicago Press, 1996), 133–76.

25. The best work on these processes is Thomas Simpson, *American Universities and the Birth of Modern Mormonism, 1867–1940* (Chapel Hill: University of North Carolina Press, 2016), especially 28–54.

26. T. J. Jackson Lears, *No Place of Grace: Antimodernism and the Transformation of American Culture, 1880–1920* (Chicago: University of Chicago Press, 1994); Benedict Anderson, "Staging Antimodernism in the Age of High

Capitalist Nationalism," in *Antimodernism and Artistic Experience: Policing the Boundaries of Modernity*, ed. Lynda Jessup, 97–103 (Toronto: University of Toronto Press, 2001).

27. Smith and Stewart, *Life of Joseph Fielding Smith*, 123–35. Fielding Smith claims that his father asked him to respond to Evans in Smith to Douglas Smith, May 22, 1945.

28. For his service, see Smith and Stewart, *Life of Joseph Fielding Smith*, 333–36, and Gibbons, *Joseph Fielding Smith*, 356, 368.

29. Joseph Fielding Smith to David O. McKay, December 17, 1920, David O. McKay Papers, box 1, folder 11, Marriott Library Special Collections. The volume published was Joseph Fielding Smith, *Essentials in Church History* (Salt Lake City: Deseret, 1922).

30. Joseph Fielding Smith, *The Way to Perfection: Short Discourses on Gospel Themes* (Salt Lake City: Genealogical Society of Utah, 1931); Joseph Fielding Smith, *The Progress of Man* (Salt Lake City: Genealogical Society of Utah, 1936); *Topical Outlines to the Way to Perfection* (Salt Lake City: Genealogical Society of Utah, 1932), 1.

31. Joseph Fielding Smith, *Answers to Gospel Questions*, ed. Joseph Fielding Smith Jr., 5 vols. (Salt Lake City: Deseret, 1966); Joseph Fielding Smith, *Man: His Origin and Destiny* (Salt Lake City: Deseret, 1954).

32. The standard work describing progressivism as an impulse toward standardization is Robert Wiebe, *The Search for Order: 1877–1920* (New York: Macmillan, 1966). On this process in LDS theology, see Thomas Alexander, "The Reconstruction of Mormon Doctrine," *Sunstone* 5, no. 4 (July–August 1980): 24–33.

33. On the idea of fundamentalists as religious systematizers, modern in that sense, I draw on Timothy Gloege, *Guaranteed Pure: The Moody Bible Institute, Business, and the Making of Modern Evangelicalism* (Chapel Hill: University of North Carolina Press, 2016), and George Marsden, *Fundamentalism and American Culture* (New York: Oxford University Press, 2006), 212–21.

34. Joseph Fielding Smith, *Signs of the Times*, exp. ed. (Salt Lake City: Deseret, 1952).

35. Joseph Fielding Smith to Rudger Clawson and Members of the Council of Apostles, January 14, 1931, David Buerger Papers, box 10, folder 15, Marriott Library Special Collections.

36. Gary Bergera and Ron Priddis, *Brigham Young University: A House of Faith* (Salt Lake City: Signature, 1985), 131–73; Simpson, *American Universities*, 92–122; Casey P. Griffiths, "The Chicago Experiment Finding the Voice and Charting the Course of Religious Education in the Church," *BYU Studies* 49, no. 4 (2010): 91–130; Mary Bradford, *Lowell Bennion: Teacher, Counselor, Humanitarian* (Salt Lake City: Dialogue Foundation, 1995), 126–54.

37. Gibbons, *Joseph Fielding Smith*, 436–39.

38. "These Times: Organization," *Improvement Era*, April 1970, 76.

39. On correlation, see Gregory Prince and William Robert Wright, *David O. McKay and the Rise of Modern Mormonism* (Salt Lake City: University of Utah Press, 2005), 139–59; Matthew Bowman, "Zion: The Progressive Roots of Mormon Correlation," in *Directions for Mormon Studies in the Twenty-First Century*, ed. Patrick Mason, 20–32 (Salt Lake City: University of Utah Press, 2016).

40. Joseph Fielding Smith, "To the Saints in Great Britain," *Ensign*, September 1971, 2.

41. Ezra Taft Benson, "God's Hand in Our Nation's History," December 30, 1984, box 46, folder 4, Richard D. Poll Papers, Marriott Library Special Collections.

Chapter 2. Texts

1. Portions of this diary entry are reprinted in Joseph Fielding Smith Jr. and John Stewart, *The Life of Joseph Fielding Smith* (Salt Lake City: Deseret, 1972), 96–98, and Francis M. Gibbons, *Joseph Fielding Smith: Gospel Scholar, Prophet of God* (Salt Lake City: Deseret, 1992), 89–90.

2. On the history and methodology of proof-texting, see Jane Kanarek, *Biblical Narrative and the Formation of Rabbinical Law* (New York: Cambridge University Press, 2014), 84–86; Brian Malley, *How the Bible Works: An Anthropological Study of Evangelical Biblicism* (Walnut Creek, CA: AltaMira, 2004), 78–80.

3. This passage is quoted only in Smith and Stewart, *Life of Joseph Fielding Smith*, 97.

4. The term *scripturalization* is Vincent Wimbush's, as discussed especially in his "Scripturalizing: Analytical Wedge for a Critical History of the Human," in *Scripturalizing the Human: The Written as the Political*, ed. Vincent Wimbush, 1–19 (New York: Routledge, 2015). I also draw on Seth Perry, *Bible Culture and Authority in the Early United States* (Princeton, NJ: Princeton University Press, 2018), 5–15, and Wilfred Cantwell Smith, *What Is Scripture? A Comparative Approach* (Minneapolis: Fortress, 1993), 1–21.

5. See, for instance, Joseph Fielding Smith, *Doctrines of Salvation: Sermons and Writings of Joseph Fielding Smith*, comp. Bruce R. McConkie, 3 vols. (Salt Lake City: Bookcraft, 1954–56), 1: 3; 1: 14; 1: 60; 1: 174.

6. On New Testament proof-texting, see Jeremy Punt, "Paul, Hermeneutics, and the Scriptures of Israel," *Neotestimentica* 30, no. 2 (1996): 377–425; E. P. Sanders, *Comparing Judaism and Christianity: Common Judaism, Paul, and the Inner and Outer in the Study of Religion* (Minneapolis: Fortress, 2016), 219–30; Lisa Gordis, *Opening Scripture: Bible Reading and Interpretive Authority in Puritan New England* (Chicago: University of Chicago Press, 2003), 88–90, 183–85.

7. Philip Barlow, *Mormons and the Bible: The Place of the Latter-day Saints in American Religion* (New York: Oxford University Press, 1991), 84; Orson Pratt, *Divine Authenticity of the Book of Mormon* (Liverpool, UK: R. James, 1850), 6: 91–92. Orson Pratt, "Things of God Revealed Only by the Spirit of God," *Journal of Discourses* 15 (London: Albert Carrington, 1873), 178–79.

8. Joseph Fielding Smith, "Asahel Smith of Topsfield, with Some Account of the Smith Family," *Historical Collections of the Topsfield Historical Society* 8 (1902): 90, 92.

9. On common sense and perspicuity, see Mark Noll, *America's God: From Jonathan Edwards to Abraham Lincoln* (New York: Oxford University Press, 2002), 367–89; George M. Marsden, "Everyone One's Own Interpreter: The Bible, Science and Authority in Mid-Nineteenth Century America," in *The Bible in America: Essays in Cultural History*, ed. Nathan O. Hatch and Mark Noll, 79–101 (New York: Oxford University Press, 1982); Jonathan Hill, *Faith in the Age of Reason* (Oxford, UK: Lion House, 2004), 110–12.

10. Brigham Young, "Object of the Express Carrying Company," *Journal of Discourses*, 26 vols. (Liverpool, UK: S. W. Richards, 1857), 4: 305. See the discussion of Kimball in Nathan O. Hatch, *The Democratization of American Christianity* (New Haven, CT: Yale University Press, 1991), 133–41.

11. Benjamin B. Warfield and Archibald A. Hodge, "Inspiration," *Presbyterian Review* 6 (April 1881): 225–60, is the classic statement of what came to be known as the doctrine of biblical inerrancy. See also Mark Noll, *Between Faith and Criticism: Evangelicals, Scholarship and the Bible in America* (San Francisco: Harper and Row, 2006), 11–32, and George Marsden, *Fundamentalism and American Culture* (New York: Oxford University Press, 2006), 111–13.

12. Malley, *How the Bible Works*; Susan Friend Harding, *The Book of Jerry Falwell: Fundamentalist Language and Politics* (Princeton, NJ: Princeton University Press, 2000); James Bielo, "On the Failure of Meaning: Bible Reading in the Anthropology of Christianity," *Culture and Religion* 9, no. 1 (March 2008): 1–28.

13. Richard Gaillardetz, *When the Magisterium Intervenes: The Magisterium and Theologians in Today's Church* (Collegeville, MN: Liturgical Press, 2012), vii–xiv.

14. Gibbons, *Joseph Fielding Smith*, 83.

15. The letter is transcribed in Smith and Stewart, *Life of Joseph Fielding Smith*, 95, and Gibbons, *Joseph Fielding Smith*, 84, though the latter has the word as "wiggle."

16. John Nelson Darby, *On the Operations of the Spirit of God* (London: W. H. Broom, 1865), 114; John Nelson Darby, *Lectures on the Second Coming* (London: W. H. Broom, 1868), 2.

17. Smith and Stewart, *Life of Joseph Fielding Smith*, 104–5.

18. Richard Poll, "Notes on a Conversation with President Joseph Fielding Smith in His Office, 11:30 am, Wednesday, December 29, 1954," box 10, folder 13, David Buerger Papers, Special Collections, J. Willard Marriott Library, University of Utah. Hereafter Marriott Library Special Collections.

19. Fielding Smith recounts his father's request that he write in response to Evans in Joseph Fielding Smith to Douglas Smith, May 22, 1945, Joseph Fielding Smith Family Correspondence, MS 14132, Church of Jesus Christ of Latter-day Saints History Library and Archives, Salt Lake City, Utah. Hereafter Church History Library and Archives.

20. Joseph Fielding Smith, *Blood Atonement and the Origins of Plural Marriage: Correspondence between Elder Joseph F. Smith, Jr., and Mr. Richard C. Evans* (Independence, MO: Zion's Printing and Publishing, 1905), 14, 26.

21. Smith, *Blood Atonement*, 12.

22. Joseph Fielding Smith, *Origin of the "Reorganized Church" and the Question of Succession* (Salt Lake City: Skelton, 1907), 102.

23. Fielding Smith, *Origin of the "Reorganized Church,"* 32.

24. Benjamin B. Warfield, *The Inspiration and Authority of the Bible* (Philadelphia: Presbyterian Publishing, 1948), 114.

25. Joseph Fielding Smith to Douglas Smith, January 9, 1949, January 22, 1949, MS 14132, Joseph Fielding Smith Family Correspondence, Church History Library and Archives.

26. Smith, *Doctrines of Salvation*, 2: 290.

27. Smith, *Doctrines of Salvation*, 3: 572.

28. Malley, *How the Bible Works*, 105–6.

29. Smith, *Doctrines of Salvation*, 1: 125–27.

30. Joseph Fielding Smith to J. Reuben Clark, September 27, 1946, 1, 2, 3, box 158, folder 3, J. Reuben Clark Papers, L. Tom Perry Special Collections, Lee Library, Brigham Young University.

31. Smith, *Doctrines of Salvation*, 3: 565.

32. Smith, *Doctrines of Salvation*, 3: 567.

33. Smith, *Doctrines of Salvation*, 3: 580–81.

34. Thomas W. Davis, *Shifting Sands: The Rise and Fall of Biblical Archaeology* (New York: Oxford University Press, 2004), 21–28.

35. John A. Widtsoe, speech, in *Ninety-Eighth Semi-annual Conference of the Church of Jesus Christ of Latter-day Saints* (Salt Lake City: Church of Jesus Christ of Latter-day Saints, 1927), 26; Terryl Givens, *By the Hand of Mormon: The American Scripture That Launched a New World Religion* (New York: Oxford University Press, 2002), 106–8.

36. Smith, *Doctrines of Salvation*, 1: 93.

37. Joseph Fielding Smith, "Address, November 18, 1923," MS 2650, Church History Library and Archives; Smith, *Doctrines of Salvation*, 3: 592–94.

38. Joseph Fielding Smith to Albert Hunter, January 11, 1937, MS 17153, Church History Library and Archives.

39. Smith, *Doctrines of Salvation*, 1: 186, 279. Originally in *121st Semi-annual Conference of the Church of Jesus Christ of Latter-day Saints* (Salt Lake City: Deseret, 1950), 11–12.

40. Joseph Fielding Smith, *Man: His Origin and Destiny* (Salt Lake City: Deseret, 1954), 418, 33–34.

41. John Sillito, *B. H. Roberts: A Life in the Public Arena* (Salt Lake City: Signature, 2021), 481–82; the newspaper is in box 4, folder 23, Scott G. Kenney Collection, Marriott Library Special Collections.

42. B. H. Roberts, "Higher Criticism and the Book of Mormon," *Improvement Era*, June 1911, 668–69; B. H. Roberts, *New Witnesses for God* (Salt Lake City: Deseret News, 1909) 2: 12. See also Matthew Bowman, "Biblical Criticism, the Book of Mormon, and the Meanings of Civilization," *Journal of Book of Mormon Studies* 30 (2021): 62–89.

43. John William Draper, *History of the Conflict between Religion and Science* (New York: Appleton, 1896); Andrew Dickson White, *A History of the Warfare of Science with Theology in Christendom* (New York: Appleton, 1876).

44. Draper, *History of the Conflict*, vi. David Lindberg and Ronald Numbers, Introduction to *God and Nature: Historical Essays on the Encounter between Christianity and Science,* ed. Lindberg and Numbers (Berkeley: University of California Press, 1968), 1–19; James Ungureau, *Science, Religion, and the Protestant Tradition: Retracing the Origins of Conflict* (Pittsburgh, PA: University of Pittsburgh Press, 2019), 22–103.

45. Smith, *Man*, 280.

46. Joseph Fielding Smith to George McCready Price, February 12, 1931, box 1, folder 4, George McCready Price Papers, White Library, Andrews University, Berrien Springs, MI.

47. Joseph Fielding Smith, "Faith Leads to a Fulness of Truth and Righteousness," *Utah Genealogical and Historical Magazine* 21 (October 1930): 147–48.

48. B. H. Roberts, *The Truth, the Way, the Life: An Elementary Treatise on Theology* (Provo, UT: BYU Studies Press, 1996), 298–318. On the committee's work, see Rudger Clawson to Committee, October 3, 1928, Jay Bell Papers, box 10, folder 5, Marriott Library Special Collections.

49. Smith, "Faith Leads," 148. On Fielding Smith's disagreements with other apostles of his time, see Barlow, *Mormons and the Bible*, 112–62; Richard Sherlock, "A Turbulent Spectrum: Mormon Reactions to the Darwinist Legacy," *Journal of Mormon History* 5 (1978): 33–59.

50. B. H. Roberts to President Heber J. Grant and Counselors, December 15, 1930, box 4, folder 19, Scott G. Kenney Collection, Marriott Library Special Collections. See also Rudger Clawson to President Heber J. Grant, January 21, 1932, box 10, folder 13, David Buerger Papers, Marriott Library Special Collections.

51. Roberts, *The Truth, the Way, the Life*, 216, 218, 220.

52. B. H. Roberts to Rudger Clawson, December 31, 1930, box 10, folder 5, Jay Bell Papers, Marriott Library Special Collections.

53. On this point, see Clawson to Grant, January 21, 1932.

54. Joseph Fielding Smith to Rudger Clawson and Members of the Council of Apostles, January 14, 1931, 63, box 10, folder 14, David Buerger Papers, Marriott Library Special Collections.

55. Joseph Fielding Smith to Franklin L. West and M. Lynn Bennion, March 11, 1937, box 5, folder 2, Mary Bradford Papers, Marriott Library Special Collections.

56. Heber J. Grant Diary Excerpts, January 25, 1931, box 10, folder 12, David Buerger Papers, Marriott Library Special Collections. See also Richard Sherlock, "We Can See No Advantage in a Continuation of the Discussion: The Roberts/Smith/Talmage Affair," *Dialogue* 13, no. 3 (Fall 1980): 70–71.

57. J. Reuben Clark to Joseph Fielding Smith, October 2, 1946, box 158, folder 3, J. Reuben Clark Papers.

58. Clark to Smith, October 2, 1946; the talk is published as "Our Wives and Our Mothers in the Eternal Plan," *Relief Society Magazine*, December 1946, 795–804.

59. Smith to Rudger Clawson and Members of the Council of Apostles, January 14, 1931, 14.

Chapter 3. Progress

1. John Logsdon, *John F. Kennedy and the Race to the Moon* (New York: Palgrave Macmillan, 2011); Douglas Brinkley, *American Moonshot: John F. Kennedy and the Great Space Race* (New York: HarperCollins, 2019).

2. "Moon Shots Hit by Churchman," *Daily Oklahoman*, April 26, 1962, 24; "Mormon Leader Says Moon Not Meant for Man," *Arizona Daily Star*, April 25, 1962, 1. Fielding Smith's diary entries are reprinted in Joseph Fielding Smith Jr. and John J. Stewart, *The Life of Joseph Fielding Smith* (Salt Lake City: Deseret, 1972), 322.

3. Joseph Fielding Smith to Robert Lee Echols, May 1, 1962, MSS SC 2031, L. Tom Perry Special Collections, Harold B. Lee Library, Brigham Young University, Provo, Utah. See also Joseph Fielding Smith to Orville Gunther, May

5, 1958, box 1, folder 8, David Bailey Papers, Special Collections, J. Willard Marriott Library, University of Utah. Hereafter Marriott Library Special Collections.

4. Joseph Fielding Smith, *Man: His Origin and Destiny* (Salt Lake City: Deseret, 1954), 464–65.

5. Joseph Fielding Smith to Henry Eyring, June 12, 1950, MS 396, Church History Library and Archives, Salt Lake City, Utah. Hereafter Church History Library and Archives.

6. Brett Bowden, *The Empire of Civilization: The Evolution of an Imperial Idea* (Chicago: University of Chicago Press, 2009), 31. I also draw on the work of Gail Bederman, *Manliness and Civilization* (Chicago: University of Chicago Press, 2008), 1–45.

7. Francois Guizot, *A History of Civilization in Europe*, trans., William Hazlitt (London: Penguin Press, 1997), 12, 16.

8. George Marsden describes Marxism as only the most famous of great nineteenth-century universal theories of civilization in *Fundamentalism and American Culture* (New York: Oxford University Press, 2006), 63–65. See also Thomas Jefferson, *Notes on the State of Virginia* (Philadelphia: H. C. Carey, 1825), 87.

9. Hebert Spencer, *Social Statics* (London: Williams and Norgate, 1868), 455. Richard Hofstadter, *Social Darwinism in American Thought* (Philadelphia: University of Pennsylvania Press, 1944), 18–37. The extension of evolutionary ideas to social theory is discussed in Peter Bowler, *Evolution: The History of an Idea* (Berkeley: University of California Press, 2009), 284–307.

10. Lewis Henry Morgan, *Ancient Society* (New York: Henry Holt, 1877), 60–61, 510–11.

11. E. B. Tylor, *Primitive Culture*, 3rd ed. (London: John Murray, 1891. Tylor discusses Spencer on vii; 17, 421, 21.

12. Arthur de Gobineau, *The Moral and Intellectual Diversity of Races* (Philadelphia: J. B. Lippincott, 1856), 267, 271.

13. Theodore Roosevelt, *The New Nationalism* (New York: Outlook, 1910), 244. See also Lyman Abbott, *The Evolution of Christianity* (Boston: Houghton Mifflin, 1892), 16.

14. Joseph Fielding Smith to David O. McKay, December 17, 1920, David O. McKay Papers, box 1, folder 11, Marriott Library Special Collections.

15. Peter Novick, *That Noble Dream: The Objectivity Question and the American Historical Profession* (New York: Cambridge University Press, 1988), 21–61.

16. Jonathan Edwards, *A History of the Work of Redemption* (Boston: Draper and Folsom, 1782), 130. See also Avihu Zakai, *Jonathan Edwards's Philosophy of*

History: The Reenchantment of the World in the Age of Enlightenment (Princeton, NJ: Princeton University Press, 2009), 226–39.

17. B. H. Roberts, ed., *History of the Church of Jesus Christ of Latter-day Saints*, 6 vols. (Salt Lake City: Deseret News Press, 1902–32), 1: xxiv.

18. Joseph Fielding Smith, *Essentials in Church History* (Salt Lake City: Deseret News Press, 1922), 2.

19. Roberts, *History of the Church*, xxiii.

20. Smith, *Essentials in Church History*, 2, 3.

21. Smith, *Man*, 470.

22. Joseph Fielding Smith, "The Twelve Apostles," MS 24719, Church History Library and Archives.

23. Joseph Fielding Smith, *"Was Temple Work Done in the Days of the Old Prophets?" Improvement Era*, November 1955, 794; see also Joseph Fielding Smith, *Answers to Gospel Questions*, ed. Joseph Fielding Smith Jr., 5 vols. (Salt Lake City: Deseret, 1957–66), 1: 49–51.

24. Joseph Fielding Smith, "The Apostle Paul and Genealogical Research," *Improvement Era*, April 1957, 222–23. See also Smith, *Answers*, 1: 212–15.

25. Joseph Fielding Smith, *The Progress of Man* (Salt Lake City: Genealogical Society of Utah, 1936), 21, 67.

26. Wilhelm Schmidt, *The Origin and Growth of Religion: Facts and Theories* (London: Methuen, 1931), 219; James L. Cox, *The Invention of God in Indigenous Societies* (Durham, NC: Acumen, 2014), 22–26. Fielding Smith discusses Schmidt in *Progress of Man*, 22. On Eliade, see his *Sacred and the Profane: The Nature of Religion* (New York: Harcourt Brace, 1957), 68–72; on Nibley, see Terryl Givens and Brian Hauglid, *The Pearl of Greatest Price: Mormonism's Most Controversial Scripture* (New York: Oxford University Press, 2019), 107, 139–40, 161–62.

27. J. P. Maclean, *The Mound Builders* (Cincinnati, OH: Robert Clarke, 1879), 123, 126. Fielding Smith discusses Maclean in *Progress of Man*, 42–44.

28. Maclean, *Mound Builders*, 145, 146, 147.

29. Brian Regal, *The Battle over America's Origin Story: Legends, Amateurs, and Professional Historiographers* (New York: Palgrave Macmillan, 2022), 57–58.

30. Joseph Fielding Smith, *Salvation Universal* (Salt Lake City: Genealogical Society of Utah, 1920), 3, 8.

31. The best discussion of the issue is in W. Paul Reeve, *Religion of a Different Color: Race and the Mormon Struggle for Whiteness* (New York: Oxford University Press, 2015), 106–215.

32. B. H. Roberts, "To the Youth of Israel," *Contributor* 6 (1885): 297.

33. Joseph Fielding Smith to Milton E. Smith, May 22, 1948, Joseph Fielding Smith Family Correspondence, MS14132, Church History Library and Archives.

34. Joseph Fielding Smith, *The Way to Perfection: Short Discourses on Gospel Themes* (Salt Lake City: Genealogical Society of Utah, 1931), 42, 43, 44, 48.

35. Joseph Fielding Smith to Mrs. Doyle Nunley, October 13, 1959, MS 9003, Church History Library and Archives. On Elijah Abel, see Reeve, *Religion of a Different Color*, 109, 193–97.

36. Smith to Nunley, October 13, 1959.

37. Smith to Milton Smith, May 22, 1948.

38. Fielding Smith, *Way to Perfection*, 113, 115–16.

39. Fielding Smith, *Progress of Man*, 38, 263.

40. Fielding Smith, *Progress of Man*, 263–64.

41. Joseph Fielding Smith, "Oahu Stake Conference, Sunday, September 13, 1970," MS 118, Church History Library and Archives.

42. Fielding Smith, *Way to Perfection*, 128; "Address of President Joseph Fielding Smith: Advanced Theology," June 15, 1956, box 5, folder 2, Milford Gardner Papers, Marriott Library Special Collections.

43. Joseph Fielding Smith to Douglas Smith, July 26, 1947, Joseph Fielding Smith Family Correspondence, MS14132, Church History Library and Archives.

44. Fielding Smith, *Progress of Man,* 458.

45. Joseph Fielding Smith to Milton Smith, October 3, 1948, and Joseph Fielding Smith to Douglas Smith, December 10, 1948, both in Joseph Fielding Smith Family Correspondence, MS14132, Church History Library and Archives. On early Mormon views of Native Americans, see Reeve, *Religion of a Different Color,* 75–106.

46. John Gilder Shaw, *Israel Notwithstanding* (London: British Israel Identity Corporation, 1879), 84, see also Colin Kidd, *The Forging of Races: Race and Scripture in the Atlantic World, 1600–2000* (New York: Cambridge University Press, 2000), 203–18, quote on 212. On LDS invocations of British Israelism, see Armand Mauss, *All Abraham's Children: Changing Mormon Conceptions of Race and Lineage* (Urbana: University of Illinois Press, 2003), 18–23.

47. Julius Wellhausen, *Prolegomena to the History of Israel*, trans. J. Sutherland Black and Allan Menzies (Edinburgh: Adam and Charles Black, 1885), 473–74; Aly Elrefaei, *Wellhausen and Kaufmann: Ancient Israel and Its Religious History* (Boston: de Gruyter, 2016), 61–73; Baruch Halpern, *The First Historians: The Hebrew Bible and History* (New York: Harper and Row, 1988), 19–24.

48. Harry Emerson Fosdick, *The Modern Use of the Bible* (New York: Macmillan, 1924), 24, 29. On the power of the higher criticism's ideas among American Protestants, see William Hutchison, *The Modernist Impulse in American Protestantism* (Durham, NC: Duke University Press, 1992), 89–97.

49. Ralph Chamberlin, "The Early Hebrew Conception of the Universe," *White and Blue* (December 24, 1909): 85; see also Richard Sherlock, "Campus in Crisis: BYU 1911," *Sunstone* January–February 1979, 10–16, and Gary James Bergera, "The 1911 Evolution Controversy at Brigham Young University," in *The Search*

for Harmony: Essays on Science and Mormonism, ed. Craig Oberg and Gene Sessions, 23–41 (Salt Lake City: Signature, 1993).

50. Joseph F. Smith, "Theory and Divine Revelation," *Improvement Era* 14, no. 6 (April 1911): 549.

51. John A. Widtsoe, *Joseph Smith as Scientist* (Salt Lake City: Young Men's Mutual Improvement Association, 1908), 103, 105.

52. John A. Widtsoe, *A Rational Theology* (Salt Lake City: Melchizedek Priesthood Committee, 1915), 53–54.

53. B. H. Roberts, *The Truth, the Way, the Life: An Elementary Treatise on Theology* (Provo, UT: BYU Studies Press, 1996), 240, 317.

54. B. H. Roberts, *Studies of the Book of Mormon*, ed. Brigham Madsen (Salt Lake City: Signature, 1992), 166–67.

55. Roberts, *Studies of the Book of Mormon*, 63.

56. Roberts, *Studies of the Book of Mormon*, 117, 119–20.

57. Roberts, *Studies of the Book of Mormon*, 15.

58. Smith, *Man*, 503.

59. Joseph Fielding Smith to Franklin L. West and M. Linn [*sic*] Bennion, March 11, 1937, 3–4, box 5, folder 2, Mary Lythgoe Bradford Papers, Marriott Library Special Collections.

60. Smith, *Progress of Man*, 142.

61. Joseph Fielding Smith to Douglas Smith, December 31,1943, and February 16, 1948, both in Joseph Fielding Smith Family Correspondence, MS14132, Church History Library and Archives.

62. Reinhold Niebuhr, *The Nature and Destiny of Man: A Christian Interpretation* (London: Nisbet, 1948), 280.

63. Joseph Fielding Smith, *The Restoration of All Things* (Salt Lake City: Deseret, 1973), 248.

64. Carl Henry, *Has Democracy Had Its Day?* (Grand Rapids, MI: Acton Institute, 1996), 1. On the growing emphasis on sin among American Christians of all types in the 1940s and 1950s, see Andrew Finstuen, *Original Sin and Everyday Protestants: The Theology of Reinhold Niebuhr, Billy Graham, and Paul Tillich in an Age of Anxiety* (Chapel Hill: University of North Carolina Press, 2014), 3–63; on the evangelical movement toward political conservatism, see Daniel K. Williams, *God's Own Party: The Making of the Christian Right* (New York: Oxford University Press, 2010), 18–33; Matthew Sutton, "Was FDR the Antichrist? The Birth of Fundamentalist Antiliberalism in a Global Age," *Journal of American History* 98, no. 4 (March 2012): 1052–74.

65. Joseph Fielding Smith to Douglas Smith, April 20, 1945, and Joseph Fielding Smith to Lewis W. Smith, October 29, 1944, both in Joseph Fielding Smith Family Correspondence, MS14132, Church History Library and Archives.

66. Joseph Fielding Smith, *The Signs of the Times: A Series of Discussions* (Salt Lake City: Deseret News Press, 1943), 181–82.

67. John Fiske, *The Beginnings of New England* (Boston: Houghton Mifflin, 1889), 7–8.

68. Joseph Fielding Smith, *Doctrines of Salvation: Sermons and Writings of Joseph Fielding Smith*, comp. Bruce R. McConkie, 3 vols. (Salt Lake City: Bookcraft, 1954–56), 1: 145–46; see also Smith, *Signs of the Times*, 177.

69. Smith, *Signs of the Times*, 177.

70. Joseph Fielding Smith, "Salvation for the Dead," Address, June 27, 1960, box 30, folder 12, George Tanner Papers, Marriott Library Special Collections.

71. Smith, *Progress of Man*, 168, 210, 214; Smith, *Signs of the Times*, 76–78.

72. Grant Underwood, *The Millenarian World of Early Mormonism* (Urbana: University of Illinois Press, 1993), 139–42; Gordon Shepherd and Gary Shepherd, *A Kingdom Transformed: Early Mormonism and the Modern LDS Church* (Salt Lake City: University of Utah Press, 2016), 194–95.

73. Smith, *Signs of the Times*, 156.

74. This sketch of fundamentalism relies on Marsden, *Fundamentalism*, and George Marsden, *Reforming Fundamentalism: Fuller Seminary and the New Evangelicalism* (New York: Oxford University Press, 1995).

75. Matthew Avery Sutton, *American Apocalypse: A History of Modern Evangelicalism* (Cambridge, MA: Harvard University Press, 2014), 10–22; Ernest Sandeen, *The Roots of Fundamentalism: British and American Millenarianism, 1800–1930* (Grand Rapids, MI: Baker House, 1978), 59–70; Paul Boyer, *When Time Shall Be No More: Prophecy Belief in Modern American Culture* (Cambridge, MA: Harvard University Press, 1992), 82–90.

76. Sutton, *American Apocalypse*, 51–52, 70–77; Marsden, *Fundamentalism*, 141–53.

77. Timothy P. Weber, *Living in the Shadow of the Second Coming: American Premillennialism, 1875–1925* (New York: Oxford University Press, 1979), 16–24; Marsden, *Fundamentalism*, 51–53.

78. William Blackstone, *Jesus Is Coming* (New York: Fleming H. Revell, 1908), 46.

79. Fielding Smith, *Signs of the Times*, 149, 150–54.

80. Parley Pratt, *A Voice of Warning* (New York: J. W. Harrison, 1842), 51–52; "History of Joseph Smith," *Latter-day Saints' Millennial Star* 10, no. 21 (March 5, 1859): 158. Christopher James Blythe, *Terrible Revolution: Latter-day Saints and the American Apocalypse* (New York: Oxford University Press, 2020), 14–25.

81. Fielding Smith, *Signs of the Times*, 156, 236–38; Joseph Fielding Smith to Douglas Smith, May 22, 1948, Joseph Fielding Smith Family Correspondence, MS14132, Church History Library and Archives.

82. Blythe, *Terrible Revolution*, 27–30; Underwood, *Millenarian World of Early Mormonism*, 29–30.

83. Joseph Fielding Smith to Douglas Smith, September 9, 1944, and Joseph Fielding Smith to Douglas Smith, February 9, 1945, both in Joseph Fielding Smith Family Correspondence, MS14132, Church History Library and Archives.

84. Joseph Fielding Smith to Douglas Smith, July 9, 1944, Joseph Fielding Smith Family Correspondence, MS14132, Church History Library and Archives.

85. Joseph Fielding Smith to Lewis Smith, July 17, 1944, and Joseph Fielding Smith to Douglas Smith, January 6, 1944, both in Joseph Fielding Smith Family Correspondence, MS14132, Church History Library and Archives.

Chapter 4. Orthodoxy

1. Portions of the letter are reproduced in Joseph Fielding Smith Jr. and John Stewart, *The Life of Joseph Fielding Smith* (Salt Lake City: Deseret, 1972), 99; Francis M. Gibbons, *Joseph Fielding Smith: Gospel Scholar, Prophet of God* (Salt Lake City: Deseret, 1992), 93.

2. The letters are quoted in Smith and Stewart, *Life of Joseph Fielding Smith*, 99–100; Gibbons, *Joseph Fielding Smith*, 94.

3. Peter Sedgwick, *The Origins of Anglican Moral Theology* (Boston: Brill, 2019), 1–22; John Wolffe, "British and European Anglicanism," in *The Oxford History of Anglicanism*, ed. Rowan Strong, 24–43 (New York: Oxford University Press, 2017).

4. William A. Hutchison, *The Modernist Impulse in American Protestantism* (Durham, NC: Duke University Press, 1992), 49–58, 91–94.

5. Bradley Longfield, *The Presbyterian Controversy: Fundamentalists, Modernists, Moderates* (New York: Oxford University Press, 1991), 9–28; J. Michael Utzinger, *Yet Saints Their Watch Are Keeping: Fundamentalists, Modernists and the Development of Evangelical Ecclesiology* (Macon, GA: Mercer University Press, 2006), 6–10.

6. Randall Stephens, *The Fire Spreads: Holiness and Pentecostalism in the American South* (Cambridge, MA: Harvard University Press, 2008), 136–85; Diana Butler Bass, *Standing against the Whirlwind: Evangelical Episcopalians in Nineteenth-Century America* (New York: Oxford University Press, 1995), 178–224.

7. John A. Widtsoe, *Joseph Smith as Scientist* (Salt Lake City: Young Men's Mutual Improvement Association, 1908), 9; Armand Mauss, *The Angel and the Beehive: The Mormon Struggle with Assimilation* (Urbana: University of Illinois Press, 1994), 3–21.

8. Joseph Fielding Smith, *Blood Atonement and the Origins of Plural Marriage: Correspondence between Elder Joseph F. Smith, Jr., and Mr. Richard C. Evans* (Independence, MO: Zion's Printing and Publishing, 1905), 5–6.

9. Martin Marty and Scott Appleby, Introduction to *Fundamentalisms Compre-hended* (Chicago: University of Chicago, 1995), 4–5. George Marsden, *Fundamentalism and American Culture* (New York: Oxford University Press, 2006), offers the most commonly cited definition of fundamentalism as militant antimodernism, but it does not explore the social and cultural aspects of fundamentalism as thoroughly as other work, as in, for instance, Margaret Lamberts Bendroth, *Fundamentalism and Gender* (New Haven, CT: Yale University Press, 1993), and Kristen Kobes duz Mez, *Jesus and John Wayne: How White Evangelicals Corrupted a Faith and Fractured a Nation* (New York: Liveright, 2020), 15–33.

10. Joseph Fielding Smith, *The Restoration of All Things* (Salt Lake City: Deseret, 1965), 66, 69, 192; Joseph Fielding Smith to Douglas Smith, May 19, 1945, Joseph Fielding Smith Family Correspondence, MS 14132, Church History Library and Archives, Salt Lake City, Utah. Hereafter Church History Library and Archives.

11. Bendroth, *Fundamentalism and Gender,* 13–14; Joseph Fielding Smith to George McCready Price, April 27, 1931, George McCready Price Papers, box 1, folder 3, James White Library, Andrews University; Joseph Fielding Smith, *The Way to Perfection: Short Discourses on Gospel Themes* (Salt Lake City: Genealogical Society of Utah, 1931), 200–201.

12. On the Chicago experiment, see Thomas Simpson, *American Universities and the Birth of Modern Mormonism, 1867–1940* (Chapel Hill: University of North Carolina Press, 2016), 92–121; Casey P. Griffiths, "The Chicago Experiment: Finding the Voice and Charting the Course of Religious Education in the Church," *BYU Studies* 49, no. 4 (2010): 91–130; Richard Sherlock, "Faith and History: The Snell Controversy," *Dialogue* 12, no. 1 (1980): 27–41; Heber C. Snell, "Criteria for Interpreting the Old Testament to College Youth," *Through the Years: Occasional Writings of Heber C. Snell* (Logan: Utah State University Merrill Library, 1969), 95–97.

13. Heber C. Snell to Franklin West, August 11, 1947, and Heber C. Snell to Earl Harmer, January 7, 1949, both in box 1, folder 8, Heber Cyrus Snell Papers, Special Collections and Archives Division, Merrill Cazier Library, Utah State University. Hereafter Heber C. Snell Papers.

14. Heber C. Snell to Executive Committee of the Church Board of Education, March 8, 1949, box 1, folder 8, Heber C. Snell Papers.

15. On Kent and Smith's modernist leanings, see Glenn Miller, *Piety and Profession: American Protestant Theological Education, 1870–1970* (Grand Rapids, MI: Eerdmans, 2007), 708–10; J. M. P. Smith, *The Moral Life of the Hebrews* (Chicago: University of Chicago, 2007), viii; Heber C. Snell, *Ancient Israel: Its Story and Meaning* (Salt Lake City: Stevens and Wallis, 1948), 2.

16. Heber C. Snell to Joseph Fielding Smith, June 5, 1950, box 1, folder 10, Heber C. Snell Papers.

17. Joseph Fielding Smith, *The Progress of Man* (Salt Lake City: Genealogical Society of Utah, 1936), 67, 21, 423; Joseph Fielding Smith to Heber C. Snell, May 27, 1949, box 3, folder 9, Heber C. Snell Papers; Joseph Fielding Smith to Franklin L. West and M. Linn [*sic*] Bennion, March 11, 1937, box 5, folder 5, Mary Bradford Papers, Special Collections, J. Willard Marriott Library, University of Utah. Hereafter Marriott Library Special Collections.

18. Henry Adams, *The Education of Henry Adams* (Boston: Houghton Mifflin, 1918), 355; T. J. Jackson Lears, *No Place of Grace: Antimodernism and the Transformation of American Culture, 1880–1920* (Chicago: University of Chicago Press, 1981), 286–97.

19. Joseph Fielding Smith to Heber C. Snell, June 23, 1950, box 3, folder 9, Heber C. Snell Papers.

20. J. Gresham Machen, *What Is Faith?* (Grand Rapids, MI: Eerdmans, 1946), 45, 105.

21. Machen, *What Is Faith*, 33. See also D. G. Hart, *Defending the Faith: J. Gresham Machen and the Crisis of Conservative Protestantism in Modern America* (Baltimore: Johns Hopkins University Press, 1994), 92–94; Kathleen C. Boone, *The Bible Tells Them So: The Discourse of Protestant Fundamentalism* (Albany, NY: SUNY Press, 1989), 28–30.

22. Heber C. Snell to Joseph Fielding Smith, July 17, 1950, box 1, folder 10, Heber C. Snell Papers.

23. Harry Emerson Fosdick, *The Meaning of Faith* (New York: Association Press, 1927), 282–83.

24. Snell, *Ancient Israel*, xiv, 193–94.

25. Joseph Fielding Smith to Heber C. Snell, March 29, 1949, box 3, folder 9, Heber C. Snell Papers.

26. Joseph Fielding Smith to Heber C. Snell, April 26, 1949, box 3, folder 9, Heber C. Snell Papers.

27. Heber C. Snell to Joseph Fielding Smith, March 21, 1949, and Heber C. Snell to Joseph Fielding Smith, April 23, 1949, both in box 1, folder 9, Heber C. Snell Papers.

28. Joseph Fielding Smith to West and Bennion, March 11, 1937.

29. Joseph Fielding Smith, *Man: His Origin and Destiny* (Salt Lake City: Deseret, 1954), 322.

30. Smith, *Man*, 205.

31. Joseph Fielding Smith to Douglas Smith, September 23, 1944; Joseph Fielding Smith to Lewis Smith, August 12, 1943, Joseph Fielding Smith Family Correspondence, MS 14132, Church History Library and Archives.

32. Thomas G. Alexander, *Mormonism in Transition: A History of the Latter-day Saints, 1890–1930* (Urbana: University of Illinois Press, 1996), 55; Smith, *Man*, 138–39, 157.

33. William Jennings Bryan, *In His Image* (New York: Fleming H. Revell, 1922), 125–25; Michael Kazin, *A Godly Hero: The Life of William Jennings Bryan* (New York: Random House, 2006), 139–40.

34. Heber Snell to Joseph Fielding Smith, June 5, 1950, box 1, folder 10, Heber C. Snell Papers; Joseph Fielding Smith to Heber Snell, June 23, 1950, box 3, folder 9, Heber C. Snell Papers; Joseph Fielding Smith to Heber Snell, July 31, 1950, box 3, folder 9, Heber C. Snell Papers.

35. Sherlock, "Faith and History, 34. See also, for instance, George Albert Smith to Heber C. Snell, July 18, 1950, box 3, folder 9, Heber C. Snell Papers. In Heber C. Snell to the Church Board of Education, undated, box 1, folder 11, Heber C. Snell Papers, Snell accuses Fielding Smith of wanting to "eject" Snell from his position. He claims similarly in Heber C. Snell, PhD, Interview, Everett L. Cooley Oral History Project, June 13 and October 18, 1973, 56, Marriott Library Special Collections.

36. Fielding Smith sets the date in Joseph Fielding Smith to Heber C. Snell, August 16, 1950, box 3, folder 9, Heber C. Snell Papers; Snell's note on the letter indicates "the meeting appointed was held."

37. Heber C. Snell interview, 18.

38. Sterling McMurrin, "Transcription: Heber C. Snell," 9, box 291, folder 1, Sterling M. McMurrin Papers, Marriott Library Special Collections.

39. McMurrin, "Transcription," 11.

40. McMurrin, "Transcription," 12.

41. McMurrin, "Transcription," 5

42. McMurrin, "Transcription," 43. The letter inviting McMurrin is Joseph Fielding Smith to Sterling McMurrin, August 25, 1950, box 291, folder 3, Sterling M. McMurrin Papers, Marriott Library Special Collections.

43. McMurrin, "Transcription," 37–38.

44. McMurrin, "Transcription," 40, 42. See also Sterling McMurrin, "Partial Report of the Second of Two Sessions," an account of the meeting written "several weeks later," box 291, folder 1, Sterling M. McMurrin Papers, Marriott Library Special Collections, on which this transcription evidently relies.

45. McMurrin, "Transcription," 52.

46. McMurrin, "Transcription," 51, 54.

47. McMurrin, "Transcription," 87–88. Gregory Prince and William Robert Wright report the McKay story in their *David O. McKay and the Rise of Modern Mormonism* (Salt Lake City: University of Utah Press, 2005), citing a recorded description McMurrin gave of the event in 1980 in the author's possession.

48. Fred W. Morrison to Joseph Fielding Smith, August 26, 1960, box 291, folder 9, Sterling M. McMurrin Papers, Marriott Library Special Collections. Morrison would later make a career of writing letters to the editor of the *Deseret*

News advocating a return to prayer in schools and attacking various media for promoting vice (Fred W. Morrison, "Constitution Doesn't Forbid Prayer," *Deseret News,* May 28, 1992, A7).

49. Joseph Fielding Smith to Fred W. Morrison, August 29, 1960, box 291, folder 19, Sterling M. McMurrin Papers, Marriott Library Special Collections.

50. Joseph Fielding Smith to Richard D. Poll, December 1, December 3 and December 7, 1954, box 291, folder 17, Sterling M. McMurrin Papers, Marriott Library Special Collections.

51. Richard D. Poll, "Notes on a Conversation with President David O. McKay in His Office, 11:00 am, Wednesday, December 29, 1954," box 10, folder 13, David Buerger Papers, Marriott Library Special Collections; Richard D. Poll, "Notes on a Conversation with President Joseph Fielding Smith in His Office, 11:30 am, Wednesday, December 29, 1954," box 10, folder 13, David A. Buerger Papers, Marriott Library Special Collections; Richard D. Poll to Joseph Fielding Smith, December 3, 1954, box 291, folder 17, Sterling M. McMurrin Papers, Marriott Library Special Collections.

52. Henry Eyring to Adam Bennion, December 16, 1954, box 22, folder 3, Henry Eyring Papers, Marriott Library Special Collections. Joseph Fielding Smith mentions the letter's "wide circulation" in Joseph Fielding Smith to Henry Eyring, April 15, 1955, MS 395–2, Church History Library and Archives.

53. Fielding Smith discusses his reply to Eyring's 1954 letter in Joseph Fielding Smith to Melvin A. Cook, April 21, 1955, box 22, folder 3, Henry Eyring Papers, Marriott Library Special Collections. His earlier letter to Eyring is Joseph Fielding Smith to Henry Eyring, June 12, 1950, MS 396, Church History Library and Archives.

54. Smith to Eyring, April 15, 1955.

55. Poll, "Notes on a Conversation with President Joseph Fielding Smith."

56. Smith to Eyring, April 15, 1955; Poll, "Notes on a Conversation with President Joseph Fielding Smith."

57. Poll, "Notes on a Conversation with President Joseph Fielding Smith."

58. William Grant Bangerter, "The People Who Influence Us," *Ensign*, May 1975, 39.

59. Bruce R. McConkie, "Obedience, Consecration, and Sacrifice," *Ensign*, May 1975, 50.

60. Bruce R. McConkie, "Joseph Fielding Smith: Apostle, Prophet, Father in Israel," *Ensign*, August 1972, 27.

Bibliographic Essay

1. Reid Neilson and Scott Marianno, "True and Faithful: Joseph Fielding Smith as Mormon Historian and Theologian," *BYU Studies* 57, no. 1 (2018):

1–59, is the most impressive example of having done so, surveying Fielding Smith's entire publishing career.

2. Joseph Fielding Smith, "Asahel Smith of Topsfield, with Some Account of the Smith Family," *Historical Collections of the Topsfield Historical Society* 8 (1902): 87–101.

3. Joseph Fielding Smith, "The Hundredth Anniversary of the Mormon Church," *Arrowhead*, March 1930.

4. Smith, "Asahel Smith of Topsfield," 87.

5. Joseph Fielding Smith, *Blood Atonement and the Origins of Plural Marriage: Correspondence between Elder Joseph F. Smith, Jr., and Mr. Richard C. Evans* (Salt Lake City: Deseret News Press, 1905); *The "Reorganized" Church vs. Salvation for the Dead* (Salt Lake City: Missions of the Church of Jesus Christ of Latter-day Saints, 1905); *Origin of the "Reorganized" Church and the Question of Succession* (Salt Lake City: Skelton, 1907).

6. Smith, *Blood Atonement*, 40–41, 60–63; Smith, *Origin of the "Reorganized" Church*, 86–90.

7. Smith, *Origin of the "Reorganized" Church*, 112–14, 86, 120.

8. Joseph Fielding Smith, *Essentials in Church History* (Salt Lake City: Deseret News Press, 1922); Joseph Fielding Smith, *Life of Joseph F. Smith, Sixth President of the Church of Jesus Christ of Latter-day Saints* (Salt Lake City: Deseret News Press, 1938); Joseph Fielding Smith, *Church History and Modern Revelation*, 4 vols. (Salt Lake City: Deseret News Press, 1946–49).

9. Joseph Fielding Smith, *The Way to Perfection. Short Discourses on Gospel Themes* (Salt Lake City: Genealogical Society of Utah, 1931); Joseph Fielding Smith, *The Progress of Man* (Salt Lake City: Genealogical Society of Utah, 1936).

10. Joseph Fielding Smith, *The Signs of the Times: A Series of Discussions* (Salt Lake City: Deseret News Press, 1943; exp. ed., 1952).

11. Joseph Fielding Smith, *Man: His Origin and Destiny* (Salt Lake City: Deseret, 1954).

12. Smith, *Man*, 55.

13. Joseph Fielding Smith, *Salvation Universal* (Salt Lake City: Genealogical Society of Utah, 1912); Joseph Fielding Smith, *Elijah the Prophet and His Mission* (Salt Lake City: Genealogical Society of Utah, 1924).

14. Joseph Fielding Smith, *Take Heed to Yourselves*, ed. Joseph Fielding Smith Jr. (Salt Lake City: Deseret, 1966); Joseph Fielding Smith, *Seek Ye Earnestly*, ed. Joseph Fielding Smith Jr. (Salt Lake City: Deseret, 1970).

15. Joseph Fielding Smith, *Answers to Gospel Questions*, ed. Joseph Fielding Smith Jr., 5 vols. (Salt Lake City: Deseret Book, 1966); Joseph Fielding Smith, *Doctrines of Salvation: Sermons and Writings of Joseph Fielding Smith*, ed. Bruce R. McConkie, 3 vols. (Salt Lake City: Bookcraft, 1954–56).

16. Smith, *Answers to Gospel Questions*, 1: 30, 4: 30.

17. Joseph Fielding Smith, ed., *Teachings of the Prophet Joseph Smith* (Salt Lake City: Deseret News Press, 1938).

18. Smith, *Teachings of the Prophet Joseph Smith*, 3.

Index

Matthew Bowman is Howard W. Hunter Chair of Mormon Studies at Claremont Graduate University, with a joint appointment as an associate professor of history and religion. His books include *Christian: The Politics of a Word in America*.

The University of Illinois Press
is a founding member of the
Association of University Presses.

_____

University of Illinois Press
1325 South Oak Street
Champaign, IL 61820-6903
www.press.uillinois.edu